Stand Up!

75 Young Activists Who Rock the World And How You Can, Too!

Edited and introduced by
John Schlimm

Published by
Publishing Syndicate

PO Box 607
Orangevale California 95662
www.PublishingSyndicate.com

Stand Up!

75 Young Activists Who Rock the World And How You Can, Too!

First Edition September 2013

Copyright 2013 by Publishing Syndicate LLC

Edited and introduced by John Schlimm

Cover and book design by Publishing Syndicate
Cover art: Allison Carmichael

Published by
Publishing Syndicate
PO Box 607
Orangevale California 95662

www.PublishingSyndicate.com
www.Facebook.com/PublishingSyndicate
Twitter: @PublishingSynd

Print Edition ISBN: 978-0-9850602-9-9
Library of Congress Control Number 2013907711

Printed in Canada

To all the young people out
there wondering what is
possible in this world—
here is the answer . . .

This Book Rocks!

"*Stand Up!* is a true testament to the power of youth. Young people like the ones included in this book have some brilliant ideas—not to mention a fresh perspective—and if we don't take the time to listen to them, we're doing children and our children's children a huge disservice. I am honored that Lindsey Eaton—a young woman with an intellectual disability—and Best Buddies are included."
~ **Anthony K. Shriver, founder and chairman of Best Buddies International**

"*Stand Up!* is an inspiring book. John Schlimm has showcased different organizations, groups and foundations in a way that makes your heart feel good. As I read the many stories of people taking negatives and turning them into positives, it resonated with me, as that is why I created my foundation and our motto, "Just Ask Yourself to Care!" I have always been a true believer in hope and looking at the glass half full, even when your glass is running on empty."
~ **Jaycee Dugard, founder of The JAYC Foundation and author of**
A Stolen Life

"*Stand Up!* is a celebration of some of the most inspiring young minds working to make a difference in our world, but it also serves as a guide that empowers readers with the knowledge that their voices and actions can also make a difference. I applaud these young heroes for choosing to make this world a little better for all of us."
~ **Dr. Lisa Masterson, co-host of CBS's** *The Doctors***, founder of Maternal Fetal Care International and "Champion" for the UN Foundation's Girl Up**

"*Stand Up!* is a handbook for the next generation of leaders—a blueprint for activating, motivating and taking action. Each of these visionary 'superheroes' has figured out the best way to use their voices and talents to serve the community and make the world a better place."
~ **Robin L. Bronk, CEO of The Creative Coalition**

"*Stand Up!* profiles many young energetic people who will make the world a better place. It will inspire many young people to take the initiative to do a project that will make a real difference in people's lives."
~ **Temple Grandin, author of** *Thinking in Pictures* **and** *The Autistic Brain*

"*Stand Up!* is an important and inspiring handbook for young people (and all of us), written by young people who are on the frontlines of today's most pressing issues, causes and crises. I'm proud to have Grassroot Soccer represented in *Stand Up!* through the incredible story written by Grassroot Soccer Zambia program coordinator David Kapata."
~ **Ethan Zohn, co-founder of Grassroot Soccer and winner of CBS's**
Survivor: Africa

"When my father, Ted Turner, created *Captain Planet and the Planeteers*, he said, 'Our children can inherit a legacy of wastefulness, or an action plan that can save our planet.' The young environmentalists and activists featured in *Stand Up!* are real-life examples of what will be required for us to create long-lasting, sustainable solutions for our world and all the species who share it. I am inspired and delighted by their courage, vision and tenacity."
~ **Laura Turner Seydel, chairperson of Captain Planet Foundation**

"The courage, compassion and vision of the young people featured in *Stand Up!* should inspire everyone, regardless of age, to champion for a world of equality, respect and inclusion for all. I am in awe of the ingenuity and bravery of today's youth leaders: many have stared down prejudice, bullying and stigma to change schools and communities for the better. My hope is that these stories will embolden bystanders to become up-standers. I am especially proud of those in this book who have advocated, in their own ways, for people with intellectual disabilities. Through Special Olympics programs such as Project UNIFY and Unified Sports, we seek to create a 'Unified Generation' where we will Play Unified to Live Unified, and where we only see different abilities, not disabilities. Sports is but one path to changing the world. As this book shows, the needs of our world are great, but the collective power of our youth to solve the issues that face us is greater. Lead on!"
~ **Timothy P. Shriver, Ph.D., chairman and CEO of Special Olympics**

"Just like in our kid-created, award-winning *Amazing Kids! Magazine, Stand Up!* echoes the inspired and passionate voices of young people who are determined to make the world a better place for all of us. These young activists, many of whom have been previously featured as our 'Amazing Kids! of the Month,' aren't only the leaders of tomorrow, but are already forging a bright path of compassion, hard work and public service today."
~ **Alyse Rome, founder and president of Amazing Kids! and** *Amazing Kids! Magazine*

"*Stand Up!* is prime real estate for the world's best and brightest young activists who have mastered the intersection of entrepreneur and humanitarian. No matter the mission, the secret to making a difference in the world is right here on these pages."
~ **Barbara Corcoran, star of ABC's** *Shark Tank,* **real estate contributor to NBC's** *TODAY Show* **and founder of The Corcoran Group**

"*Stand Up!* reminds us that young people are our greatest treasure. Delaitre Hollinger, the Little Brother to our 2012 Big Brother of the Year Brent Hartsfield, is a great example. We are honored that *Stand Up!* introduces Delaitre and Big Brothers Big Sisters to readers who are looking for ways to invest in children, families and communities."
~ **Charles Pierson, president and CEO of Big Brothers Big Sisters of America**

"*Stand Up!* gives each one of us a bright, positive and fresh new way to look at tomorrow while making a difference today. These talented and driven young activists selflessly extend a helping hand with the message that anyone anywhere can change this planet for the better and make our world a better place to live in. I applaud Charles Maceo and City Hearts, as well as all the other activists and organizations showcased in this fantastic book."
~ **Max Adler, actor ("Dave Karofsky" on Fox Broadcasting's *Glee*) and international spokesperson for City Hearts: Kids Say "Yes" to the Arts**

"Teens know better than anyone else how to make activism fun, loud and impactful—it's time we listen! So glad to see a bunch of them here in one book!"
~ **Nancy Lublin, CEO and "Chief Old Person" at DoSomething.org**

"Much is written these days about the remarkable young social entrepreneurs who have sprung up around the globe. *Stand Up!* is an unique collection where 75 of them vividly describe in their own words what they've done, why they've done it and what they hope to achieve."
~ **Howard Gardner, Hobbs professor of Cognition and Education at the Harvard Graduate School of Education and director of the Good Project**

"Changing the world begins with a vision for a different future, requires optimism that the vision can be realized and demands effort to make the change manifest. *Stand Up!* offers all three ingredients by telling the stories of young people undeterred by the magnitude of inequality because they recognize no injustice can stand once they have organized to eliminate it."
~ **Melissa Harris-Perry, host of MSNBC's *The Melissa Harris-Perry Show*, professor of political science and founding director of The Anna Julia Cooper Project on Gender, Race, and Politics in the South at Tulane University**

"If there was ever a question in your mind about where this world is headed, the young activists in *Stand Up!* are loudly and clearly providing the answer: Onward and upward! These leaders, many at the helm of their own nonprofits and movements, have created an important blueprint for young people everywhere who seek to use their talents and skills to make the world a better place."
~ **Dr. Randal Pinkett, chairman and CEO of BCT Partners, author of *Campus CEO* and winner of NBC's *The Apprentice***

"*Stand Up!* is a valentine to all those who believe in the power of young people. If you've ever doubted that the world is changing for the better, allow your heart to fill with these inspiring stories of youthful creativity, grit and determination. Reading this book will make you want to stand up—and cheer!"
~ **Alex Sanchez, Lambda award-winning author of *Rainbow Boys* and *Boyfriends with Girlfriends***

"When I was a kid, I was playing video games. The young people in *Stand Up!* are saving lives and the planet! I saved lives, too, but they were mostly from aliens and dragons. Still, I think we both did some important work."
~ **Joel Stein, humorist, author and columnist for *TIME* magazine**

"*Stand Up!* is another testament to the power of youth to change the world—full of inspiring stories of how the generation of tomorrow is making a positive difference today."
~ **Philippe Cousteau, president and co-founder of EarthEcho International, host of CNN International's *Going Green* and co-author of *Going Blue* and *Make a Splash!***

"People of all ages will be riveted by the compelling stories in *Stand Up!* These inventive and resourceful, young problem solvers unleash hundreds of ideas that will inspire us to put our passion into action."
~ **Wendy Lesko, president of Youth Activism Project and School Girls Unite**

"If you want to look goodness, decency and humanity in the eye, look no further than the wonderful young adults profiled in *Stand Up!* Amongst these inspiring stories and seriously gifted young people is Tanner Smith, who was featured on my show for his dedication to hospitalized children through his non-profit, Tanner's Totes. At an age when many get a pass for being self-centered, Tanner and the other young adults showcased here demonstrate all that can be accomplished when we deliberately set out to make a positive change."
~ **Vern Yip, host of HGTV's *Deserving Design with Vern Yip*, judge for HGTV's *Design Star* and founder of Vern Yip Designs**

"Society, as we live it in this epoch of uncertainty, has embraced the story of 'goodness.' And, nobody is living it out more than the millennium generation. Schlimm's delicious collection of stories in *Stand Up!* really inspires one's hope for humanity's future."
~ **Watts Wacker, founder and CEO of FirstMatter, futurist and author**

"*Stand Up!* reminds oldsters of how wrong we were when we used to say that youth is wasted on the young, especially when we read the extraordinary accomplishments of today's youngsters."
~ **Shirley M. Hufstedler, the first United States Secretary of Education**

"The way these remarkable young change makers use social networks, new technologies and old-fashioned hard work to transform society is both inspiring and instructive. If we could infuse their energy, passion and optimism into this entire generation, we would solve the world's problems. Read *Stand Up!* and get inspired!"
~ **Dave Boyce, co-founder and "Customer Experience Officer" of Fundly**

"Young activists today are not only lighting up the four corners of the globe with their humanitarian work and public service, now in *Stand Up!* they inspire, challenge and show other young people that changing the world begins with each one of us taking a step forward!"
~ **Tavis Smiley, broadcaster, author and philanthropist**

"I've learned from FoodCorps service members and the students they teach that you're never too young to make a big impact in your community. *Stand Up!* tells the stories of young leaders who have tackled some of our society's most challenging issues, with no fears of failure and a buoyant optimism that is infectious and inspiring. These young leaders are showing how mentors aren't always our elders. They're 'mentoring up'!"
~ **Debra Eschmeyer, co-founder of FoodCorps and recipient of the James Beard Foundation Leadership Award**

"John Schlimm marvelously illuminates the true 'other' side of youth today, showcasing them as engaged, philanthropic and groundbreaking new activists. As the co-founders of the World of Children Award, we discovered, recognized and funded many of the young people featured here, and we know them to be wise beyond their years and committed beyond their peers: Talia Y. Leman, Ryan Hreljac, Kyle Weiss, Dallas Jessup, Ashlee Smith and Alex Scott. At the World of Children Award, we believe the future is in good hands, namely those featured right here in Schlimm's carefully researched and beautifully presented work."
~ **Harry Leibowitz and Kay Isaacson-Leibowitz, co-founders of the World of Children Award**

"Deeply heartwarming and inspiring. *Stand Up!* is proof that humanitarianism truly has no minimum age requirement!"
~ **Lisa Alter, Arielle Alter Confino and Jordana Alter Confino, co-founders of Girls Learn International**

"*Stand Up!* is refreshing proof of the impact one person can have when they advance a cause in which they believe. It is an inspirational read for activists young and old—those who are agents of positive change seeking the world in which they want to live."
~ **The Right Honourable Paul Martin, Former Prime Minister of Canada**

"We hear so much about the folly of youth, and not enough about the wisdom, vision and strength. It is all clearly there, if we pay attention and give our young people the space they need to work it through. This very real and very encouraging testament is a joyful, inspiring reminder of the possible."
~ **Mollie Katzen, author of the *Moosewood Cookbook* and *The Heart of the Plate: Vegetarian Recipes for a New Generation***

"*Stand Up!* is a groundbreaking call to action by young people who are championing the notion that each one of us has the unique power to change the world for the better. This book proves that the future is, indeed, very bright."
~ **Amanda Hearst, founder and chair of The Humane Society of the United States' Friends of Finn and executive board member of Riverkeeper**

"Wow! My faith in the future is restored by these young people and how they are trying to repair a broken world. Every reader, young or old, will be inspired to do more after reading *Stand Up!*"
~ **Alan Dershowitz, Felix Frankfurter professor of law at Harvard Law School**

"I and twelve other Nobel Peace Prize Laureates work with youth who understand that being part of change isn't magic, it's about getting up off their butts and taking action to make the world a better place for us all. They understand that worrying and complaining about problems is not a strategy for change; the only thing that matters is what we do individually and collectively to change our world. *Stand Up!* celebrates what young people do to challenge the issues that confront us all. I totally love working with youth."
~ **Jody Williams, recipient of the Nobel Peace Prize 1997 and part of PeaceJam.org (a group of 13 Peace Laureates who work with young people to help them see they can become agents of change)**

"As someone living with learning disabilities, I know that difficult times can lead to strength. The *Stand Up!* activists will change the world with their ideas and their strength. They are an inspiration for what we can accomplish, especially if we all come together. This book is what 'owning it' really looks like."
~ **Quinn Bradlee, founder of Friends of Quinn**

"Thank you, magnificent generation of young leaders, for your passion and willingness to speak up, step up and STAND UP for the change you wish to see in the world. Your voices are powerful, impactful and harmonious. You dream and then you do. You are building a healthy and just world for all generations to come. That is your true gift! Lead on!"
~ **Judi Shils, founder and director of Teens Turning Green**

"*Stand Up!* is the ultimate stage for today's brightest and most talented young activists who are rocking the world with their good works. This is the real Fountain of Youth at its very best and most inspiring!"
~ **Taylor Hicks, singer-songwriter, author and winner of Fox Broadcasting's *American Idol***

Introduction

YOU inspire me!

It is your energy, your talents and your enthusiasm that motivate me. It is your limitless imagination, creativity and bright smile that encourage my own work as an activist. And it is your strength and courage in facing everything that is thrown at you as a young person in today's world that gives me the strength and courage to embrace compassion in everything I do.

When we embrace compassion in our lives, personally as well as at school and at work, we move the world ahead in a positive direction. When we stand up and take action, we move ourselves and those we are helping along a road that will eventually lead to places of which we have only ever dreamed.

The following stories, at their core, are about embracing compassion by using life's many gifts and challenges to help others and the planet to move forward. *Stand Up!* will take you on awesome adventures—from Africa's highest mountain peak to the rainforest; a ship at sea to a city full of puppets; digging in tasty school gardens to rocking the classroom in places like Africa, Pakistan, India, Peru, Colombia, Afghanistan and the U.S.; trick-or-treating with a mini Darth Vader to an iconic lemonade stand; building fresh water wells and soccer fields in developing nations to painting a unity mural and sleeping in a cardboard box in the snow; saving cheetahs, sea turtles and farm animals to honoring heroic soldiers; and so many other special missions of Olympic-sized proportions.

Within these pages, you will meet today's most dynamic young leaders, who started their work as young as three years old. They will entertain and inform you with stories about how they are forging the road to a better world, and how you can, too.

Stand Up! is a place where suffering, hardships, stereotypes, inequality and injustice are transformed into hope and new beginnings.

Your generation has already revolutionized what compassion in the world means: You do not see challenges, but only opportunities to help.

You do not see what's impossible, but instead declare that anything is possible. You do not see a problem, but rather a call to action. Simply put, you are living, breathing compassion at its very best!

Your generation has already moved the world ahead in this way. *Stand Up!* is my gift to you—a tribute to you and the bright future you represent for all of us.

As you read these stories and set off on your own adventures to save the world—one opened heart and mind at a time—I want you to always remember:

★ You have many gifts to share, so discover what those gifts are and use them to stand up for what you believe in.

★ You have the power to do anything—ANYTHING!!!—you set your mind to.

★ You must put one foot in front of the other no matter what, and always move forward.

You, my friend, are a superhero. And I am your biggest fan!

~~ John Schlimm

Contents

Chapter 3: Winning Teams

Chapter 4: The Adventure Seekers

Chapter 5: Tasty Activism

Chapter 6: Open Your Mind, Change the World

Chapter 7: Power to the People

Chapter 10: Putting the Cool in School

Chapter 11: Live Out LOUD!

Afterword

75 Young Activists Who Rock the World
And How You Can, Too!

CHAPTER ONE

 Giving the Gift of Awesome

When we give the gifts of love,
respect and gratitude, our lives
and the lives of those we are
helping are taken to a whole
new level of WOW!

Mission: Help Our Troops Call Home

by

Brittany Bergquist

When I was 13 years old, I was watching the morning news with my 12-year-old brother, Robbie, when we heard the story of a soldier returning from Iraq with an almost $8,000 phone bill. Our cousin had recently been deployed, and the story really hit home for both of us.

How could a man who was serving his country not be able to call his family for free? He was sacrificing so much for all of us. Robbie and I decided to do something. We cleaned out our piggy banks, which amounted to a grand total of $21. We also gathered lunch money and held a car wash to try to help this one man. But we then thought, *Why stop there?* And that's when Cell Phones for Soldiers was born.

Our mission is simple: We collect and recycle gently-used cell phones and then use the proceeds to purchase prepaid international calling cards for troops stationed around the world.

Since 2004, we have sent more than 181 million minutes of talk time overseas and recycled more than 10.8 million cell phones. Cell Phones for Soldiers receives an average of 12,000 calling card requests each week and fulfills each and every one of them! I am still amazed that we started with only a few dollars from our piggy banks and have now raised more than $8 million through monetary donations and the recycling and repurposing of used and unwanted cell phones.

With more than 290,000 troops serving overseas, the price of calling home is costly for many of our servicemen and servicewomen. For example, the average roaming fees from Afghanistan are around $3.99 a minute. According to the Center for American Progress, divorce rates nearly doubled for military members from 2001 to 2004 and have rose steadily since. Cell Phones for Soldiers works to keep families together by helping them communicate regularly during deployment. The Military Benefits Deployment Center lists staying in touch with loved ones as a top-five "how to survive deployment" strategy.

Even today, the day-to-day operation of Cell Phones for Soldiers is overseen almost entirely by me and my family. Robbie and I, now both in our early twenties, are thankful to have had our parents there to guide and encourage us along this journey. They've always been our biggest supporters and inspired us to dream big and serve our community despite our young age.

Since the beginning, we have been involved as decision makers and relationship builders. Most of our responsibilities have involved raising awareness for the charity by working closely with our corporate partners, as well as participating in publicity events. Last year, we spent our winter break from school in Germany, where we visited troops at Ramstein Air Force Base and passed out free calling cards.

The best part is that even though our original mission has been successful, we're not done yet—we're just getting started! We have taken Cell Phones for Soldiers to the next level by expanding the program's services to assist veterans. Helping Heroes Home, an initiative of Cell Phones for Soldiers, provides emergency funds for returning veterans to alleviate communication challenges as well as physical, emotional and assimilation hardships.

Helping Heroes Home provides a returning serviceman or servicewoman with the tools to immediately reconnect with their family and society. We tackle immediate needs to help them find a job, get to a doctor's appointment and give returning parents the tools to be able to reconnect with their children.

Military men and women sacrifice their safety, comfort and time with friends and family to protect our country, our freedom and our liberty. They are heroes in our society. Because they give up so much, we believe that members of the military and their families should be able to hear each other's voices on a regular basis during deployment and be supplied with the tools they need to reintegrate back into society when they return.

Building this program has been the most positive and motivating experience of our lives. Plus, we're so proud to have started something that motivates corporate and individual groups to work for the betterment of our military communities.

As long as servicemen and servicewomen continue to give so much to us, we will continue to give back to them.

Brittany with co-founder Robbie Bergquist

MAKE THE CONNECTION!

Brittany is the co-founder of Cell Phones for Soldiers. Just like her, you can find a need in your community, such as helping soldiers and veterans, and make the connection that will bring people closer together. To help Brittany with her mission, please visit CellPhonesForSoldiers.com.

A Better World by the Bagful

by

Annie Wignall Foskett

Volunteering has always been an important part of my life. My parents taught me at an early age to help others. As long as I can remember, my mom, dad, sister, brother and I have always volunteered—doing good deeds for neighbors, caroling at Christmas, raising money for special events and volunteering at church, school and in our community.

Winston Churchill summed it up quite nicely when he said, "We make a living by what we get, but we make a life by what we give."

No matter how many material things you have, your life will never be complete unless you give something back. I learned through example that it's important to think about other people who are sad or lonely or having a hard time, and that life is not only about ME. When you care about other people, it will make your own life richer and happier, too. That's why the idea of starting The Care Bags Foundation to help children in need seemed like a totally normal thing for me to do.

My own story of giving began in January 2000, when I was just 11 years old. I learned from my mom—a child abuse prevention educator—that many kids in crisis situations have to leave their homes without any of their own belongings.

Can you imagine not even having your own toothbrush, toothpaste, comb or shampoo? I LOVE kids and think they all deserve to have the things they need, so I decided to do something myself to make their lives better and easier. I put myself in their shoes and came up with the idea to fill fabric "Care Bags" with new, essential, safe, fun and age-appropriate items to help comfort kids, ranging in age from baby to 18 years old, during difficult times in their lives.

To start, I asked my mom to be my chauffeur, contacted two local children's agencies to see if they'd distribute my bags, recruited volunteers to sew beautiful fabric bags and personally met with local businesses seeking donations to fill them. I knew when I started The Care Bags Foundation that I couldn't help everyone, but I could make a difference, one Care Bag and one child at a time.

With a passion for kids, youthful optimism and a sincere desire to help others less fortunate, what began more than a dozen years ago as a small, home-based local service project has grown bigger and better than I ever dreamed possible! My project is now an ongoing, award-winning nonprofit organization, complete with its own Care Bags 4 Kids headquarters where donations are stored and 100-plus Care Bags are filled every month by my helpers and me.

With assistance from thousands of generous volunteers and donors of all ages, and with more than 200 U.S. and international distributors hand-delivering my bags, I've been fortunate through Care Bags to bring hope and tangible gifts of love to more than 20,000 displaced, abused and disadvantaged kids around the world! Using my website and the Care Bags Starter Kit, which is available by email, numerous groups and individuals of all ages and nations have been inspired to adopt my idea and have implemented similar projects of their own. This is great because it has allowed many others to also know the joy of giving and is helping to bring smiles to the faces of countless more kids across the globe.

My volunteer work has taught me so much! It's helped me to be more thankful for the family and good life I have. I've learned if a community works together for a good cause, good things are bound to happen. And I've discovered there are a lot of nice adults and kids out there who want to help—all I had to do was ask!

I've made a ton of new friends and have gotten to meet some amazing people, but best of all, doing this has shown me just how good it feels to help others. I like to make people happy, because that makes me happy.

Knowing I've made a difference in someone's life and seeing the smiles on the faces of the beautiful kids I help is the best reward I will ever get.

It's my goal to help as many kids as I can, for as long as I can, and to encourage others to do the same. So even though I prefer that the spotlight be on the kids I help, I've agreed to tell my story for many national and international books, magazines, newspapers and TV and radio stations in hopes that others will learn of the plight of needy kids and be encouraged to help. You can help me help kids through The Care Bags Foundation by visiting my website and donating new items, making bags or finding a way of your own to bring sunshine into the lives of deserving children.

There are so many other ways that you can also help. Whether you know it or not, everyone has done something to help someone else. It could be something as simple as opening a door for another, smiling and saying a kind word, letting someone go before you in the lunch line or even mentoring a child. These simple acts of kindness can make someone else's day brighter, and yours, as well.

I think some people convince themselves that there is so much that needs to be done that doing something small won't make any difference whatsoever. But one little thing you do can really make a BIG difference to someone somewhere.

I really love kids, so that's what I like to spend my time focusing on. I do something Care Bags-related every day. I've even turned my passion for kids into my career and am now a proud second grade teacher, inspiring my students each day to make a positive difference in the world. Whatever your passion, whether it is kids or art or sports or reading or something else you love, find something you care about and STAND UP! and take action.

I encourage you all to use your time, your talents and your voice to make the world a better place. You'll be so glad you did!

Annie

YOU'VE GOT THIS ONE IN THE BAG!

Annie is the founder of The Care Bags Foundation and has proven that even little actions make a HUGE difference. You can help her to fill even more bags of hope or start a Care Bags project at your school or in your community! Learn more at Carebags4kids.org and get involved.

My Friend Mischa

by

Jeffrey Shrensel, M.D.

Mischa Zimmermann came into third period one morning, complaining of a splitting headache and double vision. A popular, funny and smart eighth-grade student at the time, neither of us realized how dramatically his life was about to change. When the school nurse heard Mischa was experiencing double vision, she was alarmed enough to send him to the hospital. After imaging his brain, doctors found a medulloblastoma, a type of brain tumor. Following emergency surgery, Mischa began the long, hard road to recovery.

Mischa spent six months in what is known as a locked-in state, aware of his surroundings, but unable to move a muscle. Slowly, he regained much of his motor functionality and was able to eat and speak again one year after his surgery. As difficult as the recovery was for him, he later recalled that the support of his friends and family made a huge difference in dealing with his situation. This point was driven home when another, younger child in the same hospital asked to borrow Mischa's *Toy Story* video.

After seeing how happy the video made the boy, Mischa gave it to him as a gift. That moment was the inspiration Mischa needed to form Kids Helping Kids, Inc. A nonprofit based in New Jersey, the mission of the group is to fulfill both the physical and emotional needs of hospitalized and recovering children. They also aid in a child's transition from hospital life to the real world, providing mobility equipment like wheelchairs, ramps and power scooters.

In its early years, Kids Helping Kids coordinated hospital visits between well teens and kids who had been hospitalized for long-term illnesses or were recovering from severe injuries. As the organization evolved, Kids Helping Kids has encouraged independent youth volunteer and social entrepreneur projects to spread awareness and raise funds for those in need. The organization also provides major funding for projects like the teen lounge created at a local hospital in New Jersey.

Kids Helping Kids started as just a group of Mischa's friends from high school, but it soon expanded to include their friends, and after a couple years, his younger sister's friends, as well. Through it all, Mischa served as leader, mentor and inspiration to everyone who got involved. From its humble roots of meetings in Mischa's living room, the group has grown, with alumni of the original group having gone on to found chapters at their colleges.

What always impressed me about Mischa was how he dealt with his health issues. He handled things as they came and let nothing slow him down. With the aid of an electric scooter, he was able to attend college at New York University where he lived in the dorms. He later became a spokesman for Pride Mobility, the company that made the scooters he used. And Mischa even took a trip to Las Vegas all by himself. Even through his recurrences, Mischa was always fairly upbeat and was never afraid for what the future might hold.

During a trip home one weekend during my sophomore year of college, I received an urgent call from Mischa's stepdad. I knew Mischa generally hadn't been feeling well, but the news that he had been hospitalized with a dire outlook hit me like a blow to the chest. Instead of catching a bus back to school, I headed into Manhattan to visit Mischa at Memorial Sloan Kettering Cancer Center.

Friends and family had gathered in his hospital room. Mischa wasn't really awake, but he could respond to questions by squeezing your hand. I shared a few private thoughts with him and told him how glad I was to have known him and been his friend. A few days later I got the call I dreaded, but knew was coming. As gut-wrenching as the funeral was, it was also a celebration of Mischa's life, and how he had managed to touch and make a difference for so many others.

Plenty of people go through life without making as big a difference in their 70 or 80 years as Mischa made in his 24 years. As for myself, Mischa inspired me to get involved, to do community service and to see how I could help others in my own way. Part of that is the reason I decided to become a physician. I recently graduated from medical school and I now plan to be out there, making a difference on my own, just like my friend Mischa.

Mischa (sitting) and Jeffrey

HELP A FRIEND!

Dr. Shrensel's story about his good friend and Kids Helping Kids founder Mischa Zimmermann shows that when you help a friend, everyone benefits from it! So help a friend today and by doing so, make the world a better place. Please visit KidsHelping.org.

Toys to the Rescue!

by

Ashlee Smith

When I was five, my family and I lost everything in a house fire. I was devastated and soon realized I didn't have my special stuffed horse. It had disappeared in the flames. That experience planted a seed that I didn't even realize at the time.

Then, when I was eight, my dad, who was a firefighter, was fighting the Angora Fire in nearby South Lake Tahoe, California. He sent my mom and me pictures of the destroyed houses. I immediately noticed that in just about every photo, there were burned toys in the yards. Just like my stuffed horse.

Looking at those sad pictures, I knew right away how the kids were feeling, and I knew that I had to help them. I told my mom and dad that I wanted to start collecting toys to give to the kids in South Lake Tahoe. They supported my new mission to help others, but they asked, "Why toys?"

I quickly replied, "What's the most important thing to kids?"

My parents knew right away what I meant. In that moment, Ashlee's Toy Closet was born.

With the help of local newspapers and TV and radio stations, I was able to collect hundreds of toys that very first day when I announced my new mission to help the children in South Lake Tahoe. I then spent the entire month of my summer vacation organizing toys, posting fliers and making sure we had what I thought would be enough toys to hand out.

While I had support from Molten USA, Inc., Hasbro Toys and Zoobies, it was still hard for me to get adults to really listen to me because I was a kid. But that wasn't going to stop me!

Because I never gave up, I was able to donate an entire semi-truck trailer full of toys to those young victims of the South Lake Tahoe fire. The day of the toy giveaway, hundreds of children each latched onto that one item that was so much more than just a toy—it was the beginning of their new lives.

One family from South Lake Tahoe stands out in my mind every day and is a reminder of why I started Ashlee's Toy Closet. A mom and her three kids came to my giveaway event. The two boys, of course, ran off to get new train sets and books, but their little sister wouldn't even look at me. I wanted to talk to her so badly because I could see she was very sad. I went over to the table that was holding piles of puzzles and I grabbed one. I handed it to her and both she and her mom began to cry.

I felt bad at first, thinking maybe I had done something wrong. But then her mom quickly explained, "That was her very favorite puzzle before the fire destroyed it! How did you know?"

From that moment on, the little girl was my buddy for the rest of the day! While my mom and her mom cried—as moms sometimes do—my new little friend and I went off together to pick out other new beginnings for her and the other kids.

That story is a prime example of why I do what I do. Seeing the smiles on faces of children, many of whom are near my age, and knowing that I am helping them to be happy again is so awesome.

Another story also stands out in my mind. In 2009, I collected thousands of toys for flood victims in Fernley, Nevada and before the giveaway day, the toys were all stolen. This was very sad to me, but I told my mom that the people who stole them must have needed them more than me and we would just start over. Because of the love and generosity of my community, once word spread of what had happened, I was able to deliver twice as many toys to the children in Fernley.

Most people would have given up after having everything stolen, but I learned from that experience and used it to help me forge ahead. Life is not always easy, and sometimes it throws you curve balls. But you have to learn from those curves and move on.

To date, I have collected and distributed more than 175,000 toys to children across the country. Ashlee's Toy Closet is a nonprofit organization determined to help every child in the country and eventually the world after disasters of all kinds. Also, we adopt local children at Christmastime and for birthdays, giving out gifts when normally they would go without.

My motto is, "Helping the littlest victims." Building on my motto, my dream is to one day have a bus that I will call "Help on Wheels," which will allow me to respond to disasters even faster.

Ultimately, I want to someday see Ashlee's Toy Closet have different chapters in different cities and be the organization that helps children turn their frowns upside down after disasters. Through this work, I have learned that something as simple as a toy has the positive power to change lives. When we all work together, it creates a very special kind of hope that spreads faster than any wildfire!

Ashlee

START YOUR OWN CHAPTER!

Ashlee is the founder of Ashlee's Toy Closet. As she mentioned at the end of her story, Ashlee would love to establish new chapters around the U.S. You can help make Ashlee's vision come true! Visit AshleesToyCloset.org for more info.

There is a Plan for Each of Us

by

Tanner Smith

As a young boy, you emulate your father. You watch how he walks, how he treats your mother, what he eats for breakfast and how he deals with adversity. Being a father is an admirable position to a son. He is everything you want to be, but at the same time, something you know you'll never quite live up to. Nothing could be truer in my situation.

My father, Craig, was a popular guy growing up. He played football, basketball and baseball in high school, and then decided to walk onto the basketball team at Tennessee Tech during his freshman year of college. After making the team, he soon realized that his dream was not to play basketball, but to become a dentist.

Dad soon had it all: A beautiful wife—my mom, Kathy—a well-paying job he loved and me, Tanner. I consider myself the pride and joy of the Smith family. I am an only child who obviously was so perfect my parents decided they couldn't do any better. (They like to say I was so bad that they couldn't imagine having another one!) Either way, the three of us formed an extremely close bond.

Then, when I was only two years old, my father received some scary news. At age 32, he was diagnosed with non-Hodgkin's lymphoma. His condition was severe, so the search was on for a bone marrow donor who turned out to be my dad's sister. The medical procedure was a success.

After his surgery and recovery, my father went back to being a dentist, I went back to being a troublemaker, Mom went back to being one of the best moms in the world and, all in all, life returned to normal. But one thing we all learned from that experience was that you must prepare your body, mind and soul for anything that life might throw at you. And throw at us it did, again!

A few years later, Dad was diagnosed with chronic graft-versus-host disease, which is when new white blood cells from a bone marrow transplant do what they're supposed to—fight foreign substances. Only in my father's case, the foreign substance was his own body.

This disease means many things. For starters, my father has no tears. None at all. He can feel like he wants to cry, but no matter how much it hurts, his body won't produce tears. Next, he has no saliva. There is nothing in his mouth to help digest and break down the food he needs to eat in order to give his body enough energy to continue the fight. Also, because of the amount of steroids and antibiotics he has been on for the past 17 years, his joints, muscles and tendons have wilted down to almost nothing. And the lung capacity my father has is roughly 20 percent of his original healthy lung capacity. Recently, due to years of related medical issues, my father's left leg had to be amputated. The right leg may be next.

All the while, I have been sitting by and watching and emulating my father. I watch in awe at how he deals with adversity. The lessons my father has taught me are priceless, and they weren't long, drawn-out, sit-down speeches he gave, but rather lessons by example through the way he has lived his life.

Throughout all of this, have I had doubts about God? Have I asked Him countless times to take it away? Has my faith suffered from this?

Absolutely!!!

But there is a silver lining in every dark cloud. The sun shines on the other side.

In fourth grade, I was given an assignment to write a paper on my three life wishes. I still remember going home and wondering what in the world I was going to pick. I had always loved dogs, but no one had ever come through and let me have one. Not my parents, not even Santa Claus. So for Wish #1, I wrote: "I wish for a golden retriever." I mean, I figured it couldn't hurt my chances.

The next wish wasn't just a wish, but a lifelong dream. I loved basket-ball. I wasn't the best, but I could go out in the yard and shoot for hours and hours. Therefore, Wish #2: "I want to be a professional basketball player."

Finally, it was time for the third wish. This wish was a passion. I had been in many hospital rooms. I had seen kids and teens going through the same things my dad—my hero—was going through. They needed a hero, too. They needed to know someone was thinking about them.

Wish #3: "I want to make kids with cancer laugh."

At the end of my paper, I wrote, "If none of these dreams were to come true, I would still want to make kids with cancer laugh." That one was non-negotiable!

Jump ahead 12 years: I have a golden retriever named Griffey (after baseball player Ken Griffey, Jr.); I received a scholarship to play college bas-ketball in the ACC at Clemson University where I was a three-year starter and a member of three NCAA Tournament teams, and I now play profes-sional basketball in Zwolle, Netherlands; and I started a nonprofit organi-zation called Tanner's Totes, Inc., which delivers tote bags full of items to pre-teens and teens undergoing any long-term treatment in hospitals.

Back when I started Tanner's Totes with my parents' help, the idea was to put fun and practical items into tote bags that kids and teens could carry during their treatments to help make their journeys a little easier. It was a real team effort, right from the beginning. My uncle, who owned a silk screening business, made up our first bags while other family and friends helped fill them. Then, my mom and dad drove me to Children's Healthcare of Atlanta so I could deliver my first totes.

Since the kids loved the bags so much, we turned Tanner's Totes, Inc. into an official nonprofit organization. My dad helped me with the necessary papers and my mom spearheaded the shopping. Our basement was transformed into our headquarters. What started out as a small family project on a very local level has now gone national. Hospitals and other groups from around the country have joined our efforts. We have deliv-ered more than 4,000 tote bags to more than 50 hospitals in more than 25 states. Our span reaches all the way to Hawaii! We were even featured on HGTV's *Deserving Design with Vern Yip.*

When I look back on my life so far, I am thankful that all three of my wishes came true. I also think about how so many of us spend countless hours dwelling on things in our lives we have no control over, rather than focusing our attention on what we can do in the future to turn a negative into a positive. I wish every day that my father had been able to dodge all of those complications, but without my father's struggles, Tanner's Totes would not have been a passion of mine. And 4,000 kids across the United States would not have received the love that's in every one of our totes. Looking back now, I know without a doubt that God truly does have a plan for each one of us.

Tanner

TURN NEGATIVES INTO POSITIVES!

Tanner is the founder of Tanner's Totes, where he turned a wish and a bad situation into a very positive mission to help others. Learn how you can transform your own struggles and challenges into something productive and beneficial for others by visiting TannersTotes.com.

Making Spirits Bright

by

Raymond Mohler

At the age of four, I was diagnosed with a rare hip disease that left me in a double leg brace for two years. Feeling fortunate that my illness was not life-threatening, I decided that I had to do something for the kids I left behind in the hospital.

To start, I took all my Christmas gifts and returned to the same hospital to give the presents to the kids who were still there. My goal was to lift their spirits since they weren't going home for the holidays. After I saw the joy on their faces, I decided to continue doing this kind of work. My next step was to go door-to-door asking friends, family and neighbors for donations so I could purchase new toys for the sick kids.

My efforts became so popular that we created a foundation. At the age of six, with the help of my parents, the Little Saint Nick Foundation was born. My initial work for the foundation caught the eye of Charles Wang, owner of the New York Islanders hockey team. Mr. Wang generously sent NHL hockey players to accompany me to visit the sick kids in the hospital. We threw a holiday party, the players signed autographs and we handed out hundreds of toys. Then we went to the room of every sick kid who could not get out of bed and we took photos with them, signed autographs for them and delivered a very special hand-selected gift to each one of them. After every event like this, we left the hospital smiling, because we were so happy to help put smiles on the faces of those little kids.

From my connection with pro sports stars, I receive very kind donations of things like luxury suites at major sporting arenas. This allows me to also take sick or underprivileged children to games where they can meet a few players and have a very special day to remember.

I eventually expanded my efforts by creating mobile entertainment centers for hospitals in my area. The entertainment center included a rolling cart, flat screen TV, DVD player, video game system and lots of movies to watch. These mobile entertainment systems can be wheeled into the rooms of kids who are not able to visit the hospital's playroom.

After seeing how happy I made the kids in the pediatric unit, I learned that there are hundreds of kids every month who visit the emergency room, and I wanted to help them, too. Since the ER can be such a scary place, I decided to donate two mobile entertainment centers for each pediatric emergency room. These mobile entertainment centers are wheeled up to the children to help ease their fears and let them focus on something fun, such as their favorite video games.

From that effort, I also developed an emergency room gift bag program for the same hospital. In each bag, there is a Beanie Baby, coloring book and crayons. Every child who visits the emergency room receives one. The coloring book gives the child something to do while sitting in the waiting room. And the Beanie Baby gives the child a friend to hold on to while being examined and gives the doctor something to talk to them about.

The Little Saint Nick Foundation also grants specific wishes to some very special kids. One kid we worked with was severely handicapped with cerebral palsy and other medical issues that required him to use a breathing tube to live. I raised money to build him an $80,000 home extension with all the modern amenities to improve the quality of his life.

One other event we have at the Little Saint Nick Foundation is called "Days of Giving." As the economy changed, I wanted to make sure every kid had holiday gifts to open and a family dinner to share. This event has helped more than 800 children to avoid feeling the economic hardships of their parents.

The work I do today on behalf of the Little Saint Nick Foundation is truly a gift I give to myself every time I have the chance to help another kid or family. I love to give back to sick and underprivileged children, because I am grateful that my illness all those years ago was not life-threatening.

Raymond

MAKE EVERY DAY A HOLIDAY!

Raymond is the founder of the Little Saint Nick Foundation where every day is a holiday. The gift of giving isn't confined to a certain day or time of year. Learn more about how you can follow in Raymond's footsteps and give the gift of your time and a helping hand at LittleStNick.org.

Soldier On!

by

Kameron "Pace" Tyson

I stood in the back of the room and listened intently. It was hard to believe what I was hearing. It was a hot July day in 2009 in New Orleans. I had accompanied my mom to a weeklong Veterans Affairs (VA) training session where serving homeless veterans was the topic of discussion.

To my dismay, I learned that when many veterans complete a VA program and are released, they often start over with nothing. Even those who are able to find a job and secure a place to live often have very little in the way of furnishings, appliances and other household goods. I was sure this was not the case back home in Dublin, Georgia.

When we returned home, I made an appointment with local VA officials and talked with them about what I had heard. They knew me as a volunteer at the VA and shared that, unfortunately, some veterans do fall through the cracks when they don't have family support or other assistance.

Sitting there in that small office that day, I knew what I had to do. But could one 15-year-old kid really make a difference? I was just a country kid who lived in a small community. I couldn't even drive yet! Would anyone take my ideas seriously?

That night, I called a family friend who had worked with homeless veterans before his retirement. I told him I wanted to help veterans in our area, and he encouraged me to move forward. That's how Soldier On, a program for veterans in need, was born.

My parents supported my efforts, and Mom approached her board of directors at Georgia Cooperative Health Manpower Education, Inc. to inquire if the project could become a component of their nonprofit corporation. They readily agreed, and I was excited. People would be able to get a tax deduction if they donated items. The next day, we went to the bank and I withdrew some of my savings to rent a storage building.

We made flyers and distributed them at various locations. My first donations were quilts from my grandmother and cookware from my mom. My friends scoured their attics for items their families no longer used. Soon the phone was ringing off the hook with offers of donations, and we were filling up the building.

Two veterans called, and we met them at the storage facility where they were able to choose some items. They were amazed that the items were free. "You served us, now people are donating items to help you," I explained to them.

A big cash donation came in, and we purchased a trailer to haul larger items. Several beds were donated, along with appliances and a great deal of clothing. We built clothing racks and rented another building.

One day, a veteran brought his wife to the storage facility. She had been living with relatives while he was on active duty. They were starting over and had no household goods whatsoever. When we rolled up the storage facility doors, she turned to me and asked what she could have. "Anything you need," I replied.

Tears streaming down her face, she chose a bed for herself and her husband, twin beds for her children, a dining room suite, sofa, stove and refrigerator. I looked back at my mom and a volunteer, and they were crying, too. I knew at that moment this would be a lifelong project for me.

When we had our first official pickup day for veterans, I was nervous. We now had four buildings full of items. What if nobody came? I didn't have to worry. We had advertised the event to begin at 10 A.M.. and end at 2 P.M. Veterans were already lined up at 6:30 A.M. Seven friends showed up to help.

The first in line was a disabled vet. He picked out a refrigerator, stove, washing machine, a bed, chest of drawers and some blankets. One of our volunteers hauled the items to the small house where he lived. When the volunteer returned, he pulled me aside. "Do you know what was in that man's house?" he asked. I had no idea. "A blanket on the floor—that's it," he told me.

We now have 26 volunteers helping with the project. As of this writing, we have served 154 veterans and their families and have raised more than $174,000 in donations of goods and $10,000 in cash donations. We had a car and a van donated, which we sold, using the cash received to further benefit our veterans.

During our second pickup day, the first gentleman in line was a Vietnam vet who was amazed at the quality of items people had donated. After he made his selections, we helped him load his car. He turned to me as he started to leave and said, "You know, son, when I came home from 'Nam, I didn't feel appreciated. I feel appreciated today."

We have been amazed at the generosity of our community and surrounding counties. In fact, we must occasionally turn down donations because of the lack of space. The local VFW has contacted me to ask for a planning meeting to discuss ways we might collaborate, which is very exciting. And I have been asked to speak at civic clubs, churches and other venues.

Our dream is to have a large storage facility so that the veterans can walk among the items to better make their selections. I would encourage any young person with an idea to step out on faith and just do it. When we meet a veteran at our storage buildings, I always receive such a blessing from their gratitude for the little we are able to do.

We should never doubt what our youth are able to accomplish. As I originally pondered my idea, I was skeptical. My father was very ill and has since passed away from Alzheimer's disease. My mother works full time and is very busy. But with their encouragement and my friends' assistance, the project has grown beyond my expectations.

After Soldier On was mentioned in local newspapers, we received checks from people in nine surrounding counties, along with encouraging notes that I read time and again. We were invited to be on the national radio show *The John Boy and Billy Big Show*, and, as a result, received checks from people in 23 states. In our small way, we have helped strengthen America, one step at a time. It is a shame for any American to be homeless and in need, but it is a disgrace for a veteran to be in that predicament.

Our buildings are again overflowing, and our local VA now refers veterans to our program. My plans to embrace the family tradition of attending Georgia Southern College even changed. Instead, I decided to commute to nearby Middle Georgia College so that I could continue with this very important project.

Some of our nation's heroes are depending on me, and I take that very seriously. To my fellow youth I say: If not us, who? If not now, when?

Kameron

GIVE BACK!

Kameron is the founder of Soldier On. His effort to help veterans in need shows how important it is to give back to these brave heroes and their families who have sacrificed so much for you and your freedom. Learn how you can soldier on with Kameron at www.VeteransOpportunity.org.

CHAPTER TWO

 ## Superpowers Activate!

What some people call
a disability is really
a very special power
and opportunity to
help others to be the
best they can be.

How I Found My Voice

by

Susie Doyens

I was born with Down syndrome. It is typical for people with Down syndrome to have intellectual disabilities and sort of look alike.

Most of my friends with Down syndrome are outgoing. They talk a lot and mix well with other people. I'm not naturally as outgoing or comfortable looking at other people or talking with them.

I have always been scared and shy. I used to never really talk. Ever. I wrote notes instead. People would talk to me and it made me feel panicky and uncomfortable. I never looked at people's faces, only their shoes. I was afraid if I said something wrong, people would laugh at me.

Special Olympics came into my life when I was eight years old. My swimming teacher, Emily, got me into my first Special Olympics competition. My whole class came to watch me compete. I was very proud to have so many people cheer for me. After that, I started doing many different sports. I noticed that I was good at them and that confidence helped me to do even better.

My favorite sport is golf. I love golf. I play Special Olympics Unified Sports golf. Unified Sports is when a Special Olympics athlete and a non-Special Olympics athlete (called a Unified Partner) play on the same team. My Unified Partner is Tom. We've won many medals. He is very supportive and very sweet. Tom makes me laugh.

But my biggest accomplishment in Special Olympics was when I became a Sargent Shriver Global Messenger. A Global Messenger is an athlete who is trained to give speeches about their experiences with Special Olympics. My area director asked me to become one because she thought I would be good at it. Everybody wondered if I could do it, because I still didn't talk much.

My first year, I gave 50 speeches! The audiences gave me standing ovations and I loved it. I have had the chance to speak about Special Olympics to many, many people. Sometimes, I speak to thousands of people at a time and I've now given more than 300 speeches and hope to keep doing more.

One of my first speeches was to a two-day gathering of Shopko store employees, which included a golf outing that took place on nine different golf courses. There were 1,500 people in the audience. The production director was so afraid that I could not do it that he went to the CEO and president of Special Olympics Illinois and my parents, telling them that he was afraid I would ruin the program. My parents told him not to worry.

When the time came, I marched up on stage. There were two huge screens on either side of me, and I had to stand on a box because I was too short to see over the podium without it. Standing on the box is what made me really nervous, not the speech. When I finished, the audience gave me a two-minute standing ovation! The director told us all that he was so amazed. He was so proud of me and let me know just how good he thought I was.

Special Olympics even made a video and commercial about my story, which was really exciting! When doing the commercial, we went to the Bartlett Hills Golf Course in Illinois. That is where I had taken golf lessons from the pro and good friend, Bob Gavelek.

We arrived at 6 A.M. and shot the commercial until 8 P.M. It was a very long day and there were periods of rain, wind, clouds and sun. The crew was always changing the setup so that the light was right and the background was how they needed it to be. My lines were easy because I was able to use my own words. There was nothing to memorize, thank goodness.

It was hard to be outside all day with all the weather, but the film crew and director, Martin Rodahl, made it lots of fun and they were really nice to me. They loved watching me hit the ball!

I'll let you in on a little secret about the commercial. I didn't really break the glass like the commercial shows. That was done by computer because the special glass couldn't be shipped that far without breaking and it was very expensive. If you watch the commercial, which is titled "Speechless," you'll see it's a really good trick.

I've come a long way. At first I was afraid to tell jokes in case people laughed at me. Now I tell jokes and they laugh *with* me.

Becoming a Global Messenger changed my life. I found out I really did have a voice. Special Olympics means so much to me—it makes me feel good about myself and it taught me I can do anything.

My life has changed a lot. I am finally happy because I found my voice. And now everyone else is speechless.

Susie

TELL YOUR FEARS TO GET LOST!

Susie is a Sargent Shriver Global Messenger for Special Olympics. In that role, she has proven that when you face your fears head-on by embracing your talents and interests, anything is possible! Get involved at SpecialOlympics.org and R-word.org (R-word: Spread the Word to End the Word).

Being Cool is Overrated

by

Arielle Schacter

Being cool is overrated. Trust me! Take it from someone for whom makeup, music and totally grown-up (read: 3-inch) heels have never helped eliminate that feeling of being different.

I mean, I've always been the girl who has funny ears, an accent that isn't quite right and who misses words left and right. Yes, the deaf one. Well, actually it's a progressive hearing loss, one that has, over the years, trickled down without warning from mild to practically profound. Caught between the coolness of the socially adept mainstream world and the isolated, uncool deaf world, I just never felt like I fit it. I wasn't all the way deaf, but neither was I completely hearing.

And so, while afraid that my disability would mark me like a scarlet letter among my hearing peers, I seized onto their world by attaching myself emotionally to what was generally hip. Accordingly, I knew I had to close the divide and bring together my two worlds. I had to eliminate the barriers of entry into the mainstream world by removing social and physical limitations for those of us who are deaf or hard of hearing. But, most importantly, I had to make hearing loss somewhat cool.

The difficulty in completely merging these different worlds is that there are some major roadblocks standing in the way of those who are deaf or hard of hearing from becoming part of the mainstream world. Some of the biggest roadblocks included a wide sense of ableism, which is discrimination in favor of those who are able-bodied. There was also a lack of proper and effective access to everyday places and services for those who were deaf or hard of hearing. And so, at first with my mother, and then on my own, I set out to fix these problems.

We first tackled the physical issues, the things that prevented individuals who are deaf or hard of hearing from receiving the same benefits in the mainstream world as those who are hearing. Noting that access was inconsistent and basically unenforced at venues such as movie theaters and museums, we helped these places comply with the Americans with Disabilities Act of 1990 (ADA) regulations and international standards. For those of you who don't know what ADA is, this law prohibits discrimination against those with disabilities and ensures equal access to all public places and businesses open to the public. I also spoke to different politicians about further administering the ADA and explained the need for access.

Though we were solving some of the issues that blocked the mainstream world from those who were deaf or hard of hearing, I realized that some of the social issues were not being fixed. These included the stereotypes associated with deafness and hearing loss, which were not altogether disappearing. Also, many individuals, especially teenagers who are deaf or hard of hearing, did not realize that they had the potential to achieve their dreams just like anyone else.

Honestly, when you picture a person who is deaf or hard of hearing, what do you envision? It's always old people, constantly interrupting you with "What?!? Speak up, I can't hear you!" (Think: Grandma and Grandpa). Well, that's not representative of countless younger individuals with a loss.

Moreover, if you try to think of prominent individuals who are deaf or hard of hearing, the list is outdated and does not get much longer than actor Marlee Matlin and Helen Keller (Newsflash: Keller passed away in 1968). Oftentimes, though, those lists are cluttered by individuals who only formed a hearing loss later in life. In fact, as far as politicians go, only three individuals who grew up deaf have ever been elected to a national-level position. Can you guess where? Definitely not the United States. Give up? They're from Austria, Greece and South Africa.

With so few strong role models who are deaf or hard of hearing, teenagers with a hearing loss don't realize that they, too, can have a successful future. Recognizing that these stereotypes had to change—to accept the individual first, and then the disability—I created a website called bf4life-hearing. The site serves as a forum to start an ongoing dialogue to change the face of hearing loss and disabilities, in general.

Bf4life-hearing's main goal is to help people—more specifically, deaf or hard-of-hearing t(w)eens—to realize that they are not defined by their hearing loss. Rather, it is a part of who they are. As such, their hearing loss should not determine either their potential or their future successes. The site is an attempt to fuse both the mainstream and the deaf worlds by breaking down some of the misunderstandings and by encouraging t(w)eens to pursue their dreams, no matter how crazy or far-fetched. It's a chance to help society as a whole overcome the limitations posed by archaic stereotypes. Can you imagine if I had seriously listened to all of the audiologists and so-called experts who told me that, because of my severe-to-profound hearing loss, I would amount to nothing?

Now, as an internationally-recognized online community and blog for t(w)eens who are deaf or hard of hearing, bf4life-hearing celebrates successes by those who are deaf or hard of hearing, challenges ableist thinking and bridges the gap between the mainstream world and the deaf world. But, most importantly, it gives t(w)eens who are deaf or hard of hearing what I had been longing for—a place to belong.

On the site's blog, which has a cool, hip young feel, mainstream issues go side-by-side with deaf or hard-of-hearing content. Current, popular topics important to most t(w)eens are given a hearing-loss twist. For example, one post was on the history of pilgrims who were hard of hearing and the roles they played in early Thanksgivings.

Also, the site uses a contemporary tone that features a texting-like vocabulary, such as "Deaf/HOH" or "t(w)eens," in order to make it accessible and more user-friendly for those who are younger and growing up with a loss. At the same time, however, the site's name, bf4life-hearing, is meant to connect all—not just t(w)eens—through a hidden bond of hearing loss, giving t(w)eens, parents and audiologists a new perspective. I am proud that bf4life-hearing has helped others around the world realize that hearing loss is nothing to be ashamed of, but rather something to be embraced. The most rewarding part of the entire experience has been receiving emails and letters from young people who comment on how the site has transformed their views on hearing loss and given them hope and the confidence to believe that everything is going to be alright.

Above all, bf4life-hearing has been personally rewarding, having opened opportunities for me such as writing for the *Huffington Post* and being honored by *Glamour* magazine as a 2011 Young Woman of the Year.

But the greatest gift I've received through my work is the ability to gain a new perspective on my loss. I see it now as part of who I am, and though I realize I am not defined by my loss, I recognize that I wouldn't be myself without it.

Arielle

THE NEW COOL IS TO BE YOURSELF!

Arielle is the founder of bf4life-hearing. She uses her popular website to show how true coolness comes from deep within when you embrace who you really are and find a way to make that work to everyone's benefit. Experience something really cool by visiting bf4life-hearing.weebly.com.

From Counted Out to Counted On

by

Hiawatha Clemons III

As a special education student, I endured a lot of ridicule directly and indirectly. Being looked at as inferior can sometimes become a way of life for a special education student. In my story, I will share what I endured for God to bring me to this point in my life where I can give my testimony.

It started back in 1995 at Brandon Middle School in Virginia Beach, Virginia where I was enjoying life as a sixth-grade student. I had developed a reputation as a class clown and enjoyed making new friends. But there was one other thing I was also known for—my temper. Whenever I felt disrespected, I lashed out. I was not even afraid to let the teachers know how I occasionally felt. Unfortunately, toward the middle of the year, I had gotten into so much trouble that I became a target, not only for the teachers, but also for the principal. And by the end of the third grading period, I was assigned to a special education teacher.

At first, it did not seem like a big deal to be assigned to a nice teacher who was there to offer extra help. However, that is when I later found out that I was labeled "emotionally disturbed." Although I still didn't see it as a big deal, I suddenly started to pick up on the jokes that students would make in reference to special education students.

At the start of seventh grade, things really got challenging. I would wait for everyone else to enter their classrooms before I would even dare to step into my small classroom. Doesn't sound like a bad idea, right? Leaving class, I would look over both shoulders, as well as down both ends of the hallway, and once the bell rang, I'd storm out of the classroom in record time before ANY students could notice me. As usual, I turned simple tasks such as going in and out of my classroom into a major production. But one day, just as I walked out of class to go to the bathroom, a student caught me off guard. And that's when I was thoroughly ridiculed.

"What are you doin', Hawata?" he asked. (Totally mispronouncing my name—a lifelong pet peeve.)

"Oh, I'm just going to the bathroom. Why?" I replied.

"You trying to sneak out of the slow class, Hawata?" he mockingly asked, keeping a straight face.

"Hey, I'm not slow, man. Just ED, NOT LD," I stated firmly. ("ED" means emotionally disturbed and "LD" means learning disability.)

"Man, whatever! That's just their nice way of saying, 'Extra dumb,'" he remarked.

Of course, I was thinking about beating him up, but that would have made the label I was stuck with even more accurate. So I swallowed my pride and let it go. Luckily, as the end of the year neared, I developed a close relationship with the compassionate Mrs. Donna Gill, who was assigned to me. Even though I had a few more visits to the principal's office throughout my years at Brandon, my mother, father and Mrs. Gill never gave up on me.

It was when I attended Tallwood High School in Virginia Beach that I reached my decision to become a special education teacher. During my junior year, I noticed how popular my special education teacher, Coach Richard Berry, was with a lot of the popular students in the school. And as some of the students were a little less judgmental once they got to know me, I came to the conclusion that special education students across the country and the world deserved more respect as human beings.

I am proud to say that when I graduated from high school, I had only been suspended one time, compared with the 10 times I got in-school suspension or out-of-school suspension in middle school. I also lettered academically my senior year, standing proudly alongside other students who had lettered for the first time, as well. I even lettered athletically in football, wrestling and outdoor track.

My decision to join the U.S. Marine Corps was based on a few things:

1) I did not have a college scholarship to look forward to; 2) My father, a retired Navy officer, is my hero; and 3) I wanted to set a new standard for my fellow and future special education students to follow.

Three weeks after high school graduation, I went off to boot camp. It was a life-changing transition for me. I must say that if I had not joined the Marine Corps when I did, I would have been a statistic like some of my classmates who were stuck in those special education classes with me. After four years and a tour in Iraq, I left the Marine Corps a different man.

After I survived another life-altering setback because of a broken engagement to my former high school sweetheart, I decided that this was the time to start a path to something more rewarding. Toward the end of my time at the Virginia Beach branch of Tidewater Community College, my veterans' counselor, Mr. Chestnutt, forwarded me an email about The Mission Continues, a six-month fellowship program that helps post 9/11 veterans transition back into society by choosing a field that they're passionate about.

Initially, I was curious before being interviewed at The Mission Continues. During the interview, though, I could sense that same genuine belief that my mother, father, Mrs. Gill, Coach Berry and a few other teachers from my school days, along with my church family, had displayed in me over the years. So I decided to go forward with this opportunity.

My fellowship returned me back home to Brandon Middle School. What a blessing! To be able to give back to the one school where I was once ashamed to be a special education student was too emotional for me to put into words. And yes, Mrs. Gill and other staff members who remembered me were there to welcome me with opens arms when I walked through the door for my first day. It was almost like a scene from heaven where God's angels were standing by the gate to welcome me in. That first day left a lasting impact on me through my entire fellowship.

The Mission Continues saved my life by allowing me to serve my fellowship back at Brandon. Throughout the course of the second half of the school year, I was fortunate enough to learn a lot about the demands of a special education teacher through my supervisor, Mrs. Robles. She and Mrs. Gill, along with many other teachers and administrators, were very wise in their views of a male role model being exactly what a lot of these students needed. And they were right.

I am grateful to some of the students who began to admire me throughout the second half of the year. But my proudest moment came during Black History Month when an eighth-grade student chose me as his hero who overcame a disability. To see my name on the front of the door with a paragraph under it nearly moved me to tears. I thank God for allowing The Mission Continues to help me serve and inspire some of tomorrow's future leaders.

In closing, to all former and current special education students who are feeling worthless, I'd like to share with you what my mother said to me as a child to help me stay encouraged. She told me: "You are not Hiawatha Clemons, the dummy. You are not Hiawatha Clemons, the fool. You are Hiawatha Clemons III, born February 14, 1984, and you are SOMEBODY."

I challenge you all to repeat this to yourself when you are feeling down or worthless: I am not (state your name), the dummy. I am not (state your name), the fool. I am (state your name), born (state your birthday), and I AM SOMEBODY.

May God bless you.

Hiawatha

DISCOVER YOUR MISSION!

Hiawatha is a U.S. Marine Corps veteran and fellow at The Mission Continues. When you take the high road and learn from life's challenges instead of fighting back, you'll discover many ways to help yourself become the best you can be. And along the way, you will also discover your calling in life. Please visit MissionContinues.org.

Adversity = Opportunity

by

Claire Wineland

There are many ways people can look at adversity. One way is to pretend it's not there, to pretend nothing is wrong and hope it will disappear. Another way is to let adversity ruin your life, to let it take over all your joy. Then there is what I do: Turn it into opportunity!

I'm 16 years old and I have an illness called cystic fibrosis or CF. Very few people know what CF is, so I'll shine some light on it for you. CF is a genetic disease that causes my lungs and some other organs to build up an overload of thick, sticky mucus. Nice, huh? Because of CF, I do breathing treatments about four times a day, and I receive at-home IV antibiotics. I am in and out of the hospital like it's a five-star hotel, and surgery is a household word (I have had 22 so far). I have had CF since I was born and at the moment, there is no cure.

Growing up, I was one of those kids who, if you put a project in front of me, you wouldn't see me again until I had created a masterpiece. Creativity got me through my childhood. I played imaginary games all the time during treatments, not only with friends in the hospital, but anywhere else I could. I let my mind wander. And I still do.

People think that because of CF, I have had a hard time growing up. But they couldn't be more wrong. Sure, I couldn't go out and play all day and traveling was hard, but that still never mattered because when you can switch on your inner child, you can make anything into a fabulous, movie-worthy adventure.

When I was young, I wanted to travel the world, I wanted to teach yoga and I wanted to be an artist with a great loft in New York City. And somehow, even though I have CF, those things seem more possible to me than you would think.

When you think *hospital*, what comes to mind: White walls? Beeping? Death? Well, all those things are there if you choose to see them. But what about friendship? Music? Art? Life? Those things are all there, too. You just have to be willing to search them out.

During my hospital stays, I transformed my room into the little New York artist's loft I've always dreamed of. And for Christmas, I went way over the top! People have told me they were actually jealous of me during my holidays spent in the hospital in Long Beach, California, because I turned my stay into such a fun adventure—into something positive instead of disappointing.

Just take a moment to think about that: Why would someone with a normal, healthy life feel any envy for MY life? Maybe because it's not about how long or healthy or normal your life is, but rather it's about what you do with the abnormal challenges and the adversity in your life. It's about how you find joy in the mundane, how you find passion in a hopeless situation.

For example, when I was 10, my friend and I threw a New Year's Eve party in my hospital room, complete with Martinelli's apple juice and shrimp cocktail. All the nurses and doctors on duty that night joined us. It was the best New Year's party ever!

I have had many adventures in my nearly 17 years of life and most of them have sprung from some of my biggest struggles. Just two years ago, my CF took a turn for the worse. I ended up in a coma and on full life support for 16 days with a one percent chance of surviving. To this day, I am the only child with CF who has been able to come off an oscillator vent and go on to breathe on my own, even though I now need oxygen. (An oscillator is a high-powered ventilator that's used to protect the lungs from any further damage. It's used when a regular ventilator doesn't do the trick.)

I don't say any of this for your sympathy—I tell you this because something amazing came from it. When I awoke from my two-week sleep, I had a new outlook and appreciation for life. I had always been excited about life in general, but now I had a service to provide and a passion that I wanted to share. I wanted to help other CF kids find their joy in life like I have. That's why

I started a foundation to do just that—Claire's Place Foundation.

My foundation isn't ME, it's not all I have to give. It's just my tool and through it I can share all I have learned. For example, I have documented and created videos on how to enjoy life with CF and live life to the fullest. Activities like this help fulfill our greater mission to raise awareness and provide education, skills and support.

I don't know where my life will lead me, but I know what's in my heart. I know that I can see things more clearly because of CF. I don't know all the answers, but I think we are here in this life to help others in any way we can. We are here to take advantage of the amazing opportunities that adversity gives us and to roll with it, no matter where it takes us.

People have always told me how I should feel about my condition. And believe me, I have felt it all: sadness, fear, guilt, anger. After all, I am only human. But I am here to tell you that through all these feelings and memories, and through all the lessons I have learned, the ones that have the most meaning are the ones filled with joy, love and acceptance.

And someday, when I am on my deathbed, the only thought I will have about CF is how amazing it made my life!

Claire

GRAB YOUR OPPORTUNITY!

Claire is the founder of Claire's Place Foundation, where she shows how the adversities and hardships in your life are simply new opportunities to change the world for yourself and others facing the same challenges. To join Claire, please visit ClairesPlaceFoundation.org.

Braille the Universe!

by

Josh Goldenberg

Hi! My name is Joshua Cooper Goldenberg, but I like to be called "Josh" or "Joshy," or sometimes my mommy calls me "Joshers" or "Poshers."

I'm nine years old. I've been blind since birth and have two eyes that Steven, my ocularist, makes for me. I go to see him every couple of months. My mommy's name is Christie, but her real name is Julie, and my daddy's name is Evan. My sister is Hannah, who is 16 and an artist, and she also writes articles.

I sometimes use a cane at stores and at school and stuff, but mostly I don't like to. I love jumping on my trampoline with all my friends. I like hiking with my dad on Sundays. I can ride a three-wheel bicycle and a Razor skateboard. I love rock climbing and my favorite breakfast is chocolate chip pancakes. I love watching football and my favorite team is the Dallas Cowboys. I got invited to go see them at their stadium and meet all the players. That was cool.

I'm really smart because I can read and type Braille, I've learned to play Mozart and Bach on the piano, I can do big numbers like 62 times 400, which is 24,800, and I can say the first 257 numbers of Pi, but I haven't practiced in a while so now I can only go to like 200.

At school, I have an aide. The aide stays with me in class if I need help, but I don't. I'm really, really good in class. In first grade, I'd get my name clipped up to the top of the chart sometimes for doing good things and went so high on the chart that my teacher had to make me a whole new color! Sometimes, it's hard to write the words and numbers on my Brailler as fast as the other kids because they use a pencil and paper, but I know all the answers.

I also started The Joshua Project Foundation to help blind people like me. Here is how it happened:

I went shopping with my mommy one day, looking for batteries for one of my toys.

Mommy said, "They're out of batteries!"

I said, "No they're not!" And then I went to touch them, but there was nothing there for me to feel. No batteries *and* no Braille labels.

I said, "Why isn't there Braille? How do blind people go shopping if there's no Braille?"

I don't remember what my mommy said to me, but when we got home, she talked with my daddy about it. They told me that we should ask the grocery store why there wasn't any Braille for me.

We went to one big grocery store because they said we could put Braille up on the shelves. Daddy talked to his friend Jennifer Bjorklund, who is on the news in Los Angeles and has the same birthday as my daddy. Jennifer came to my house and let me record my voice for TV and took pictures and stuff.

Then we went to the big grocery store and put Braille on the shelves. Jennifer went with us and talked to the people at the store. I was on TV on the five o'clock news. They said I was five years old, but I was really seven. Unfortunately, the big grocery store took the Braille down about a month later. I don't know why, but that's OK because when I later put Braille labels up at Whole Foods, they left them up and never took them down.

Jennifer came to record me for TV at Whole Foods, too, and I got put on TV again. Then some magazines took pictures of me and all of my friends at school were really excited because they saw me on TV. My teacher, Mrs. Brunner, even put the news on in the classroom so everyone else could see it. They all said I was famous, but I kept telling them, "I'm not. I'm just Josh!"

Mommy and Daddy got a call from the National Braille Press and they gave my family and me their Hands On! Award. This award is given to a person who has made a difference in the world of Braille literacy. We all flew in an airplane to Boston, and I went on live TV where the man talked with me about putting up Braille again. Then I got to put Braille up at the Boston Whole Foods, too.

There were a lot of people there this time and many wanted to talk with me, including reporters from the radio station and newspaper. They asked me a million questions. There were also many blind people there who were really happy with me that I did what I did, because now they could see all the food and stuff, too. It made me happy that they can go shopping now, just like everyone else.

When we came back from Boston, we went to Santa Barbara and I got to put Braille up in the Santa Barbara Whole Foods, too. I did it so other blind people can shop there, like at the other stores. If there isn't Braille at grocery stores, blind people will have to ask other people to read the labels for them.

I'm so happy that Mommy and Daddy helped me start The Joshua Project Foundation. We are a nonprofit, which means we don't make money from the foundation, but we have a website and we can take donations from people to make even more Braille labels for stores everywhere.

I always say, "I'm going to Braille the whole entire universe and Target, too!"

Josh

EXPERIENCE THE WORLD IN A WHOLE NEW WAY!
Josh is the founder of The Joshua Project Foundation, and he wants everyone to experience the world in a whole new way! To join Josh's effort to Braille the universe, please visit: TheJoshuaProjectFoundation.org.

CHAPTER THREE

 Winning Teams

When two or more of us join
together to create positive
change in the world,
the collective energy
and hard work of
a team is always
victorious.

The Gift of a True Friend

by

Lindsey Eaton

Living on the autism spectrum has its challenges. I have faced many setbacks, including an inability to accept constructive criticism, a lack of self-confidence and a tendency to be overwhelmed by people and situations.

In addition, my speech is sometimes hard to understand, and it's hard for me to hear people say, "What'd you just say?"

When I was little, I felt like I didn't belong, since people always teased me and I was often called the R-word (retard or retarded). My two younger sisters were always going to fun activities with their friends, while I preferred to stay home alone.

Little did I know that my life was going to dramatically change. One day, during my freshman year of high school, a teacher suggested that I attend a Best Buddies meeting during my lunch hour. Best Buddies' mission is to promote friendships between people with intellectual and developmental disabilities (IDD) and people without disabilities. At the meeting were other special education students and mainstream students. It was shortly after this that I was paired with my Best Buddy, Elaine Helton.

Elaine and I instantly hit it off from the moment we met. When I hung out with Elaine, I was always happy and smiling. She made me feel valued, important and like I was her friend. For the first time in my life, I experienced the joy of friendship. Before long, I met all of Elaine's friends, and when I'd walk around campus, people would come up to me and say "hi." I started to feel like I was an important part of my high school community.

I have some very special memories of the activities Elaine and I did together as a Buddy Pair. The two of us attended chapter meetings and events that our chapter hosted, and we also celebrated the holidays together by exchanging gifts. We had fun attending Best Buddies Arizona events, including Best Buddies Arizona's first annual Buddy Prom. At the prom, I was crowned Buddy Prom Queen. Elaine went up to the front with me to watch me receive my sash and help me put it on. I am glad she was there with me because we were able to show the staff and everyone in attendance what our friendship meant to the two of us.

On another occasion, Elaine picked me up at my house so that we could go shopping for dresses to wear to our Best Buddies Valentine's Day dance. We ultimately ended up buying matching silk dresses that looked great on the both of us. Going to the dance in our matching dresses made me feel so special and confident.

Today, Elaine and I are an ambassador/speech coach pair and have continued to grow our friendship. I recently got together with her for lunch, where we were able to talk about how the school year has been going for us so far.

Best Buddies has helped me gain my confidence and realize that I have a lot to offer, not only to friends, but also to all people. I've been a Best Buddies Ambassador and attended the Best Buddies Leadership Conference for the last few years and have spoken in front of several large groups. I now have a passion to help others with IDD to experience the freedom and confidence that I have. It is important to me that people with disabilities are seen for their ABILITIES!

I have been very involved in the Spread the Word to End the Word campaign, which is all about ending the use of the R-word. I've spoken at my high school in front of more than 2,200 classmates about the R-word and the damaging effects it has on people like me.

Here is a short excerpt from my speech:

> "When I hear the R-word, I feel dumb, stupid and just worthless. When I hear this word used, it makes my heart ache, even when it's used in a joking way, even when it is not directed

at me or someone with a disability. I know that my family and friends feel the same way. The R-word should not be a common, everyday word tossed around carelessly. The use of the R-word makes people with disabilities seem weird, dumb or different."

I'm also constantly promoting disability awareness and inclusion on Facebook. I have become an active leader and advocate for people with disabilities in my community, speaking for many people who share my feelings, but who can't articulate them.

I always tell people that Best Buddies has changed me as a person. It has helped me to believe in myself and to realize that I have so much to offer. The best ongoing part of being in Best Buddies is the strong friendships I've made and continue to make.

I am so thankful to the founder and chairman of Best Buddies, Anthony K. Shriver, and to his mother Eunice Kennedy Shriver, who founded Special Olympics. Both of these organizations are changing lives. I know this firsthand because I am a different person today, thanks to Best Buddies.

Elaine (left) and Lindsey (right)

THE WORDS YOU SPEAK
HAVE GREAT POWER!

Lindsey is an ambassador for Best Buddies International and an advocate for the Spread the Word to End the Word Campaign. The words you speak have the power to hurt or heal. Think before you speak, especially when you're angry. And even words that are meant to be funny can also cause pain. To learn more about the power of friendship and words, please visit BestBuddies.org and R-word.org (R-word: Spread the Word to End the Word).

Shifting the World, Little by Little

by

Lexi Kelley

Ever since kindergarten I have enjoyed helping others. I had lemonade, bracelet and brownie stands in my neighborhood all the time, and I would donate the money to a different local charity of my choice each time.

However, the day after my 12th birthday, my life was significantly impacted. I was in a horrific car accident, which put me out of school for a few weeks. I had to go through considerable facial reconstructive surgery, where metal plates were put into my face to support the damage that had occurred to my eye bones.

While I was recovering and in need of much love, countless people came by and showed their support by making little goodies and cards to make me feel better. I could not eat for a week, so they brought me shakes and special drinks. I spent a lot of hours in bed, so a group of kids got together and made me soft cozy blankets. I could not read, so some kids got me stories on tape. There were also many other generous acts of encouragement and kindness to help me through this rough patch in my life.

This accident and what people did to help me really made me realize that if everyone does just a little bit, we can shift the world. Being in bed for most of the next few weeks, I felt blessed to see how much the people around me cared about my well-being. It was an amazing feeling to be showered with this overpowering type of support. After I recovered, I wanted to keep that energy of giving alive.

This feeling inspired me so much that I talked with my mom about starting a group so kids could experience the power and impact of helping others and making a difference. "Kids Helping Kids" was the name I picked for the group, considering the fact that I was a kid and wanted to help other children around me. Three friends and I created our first event, a running race called "Remembering One Relay." The event benefited kids who had lost a parent or a sibling. I had so much fun, and I was surprised at the number of kids who came to participate! Those same kids were inspired to keep helping us with Kids Helping Kids and spread this positive power toward helping the community. We then went on to plan our next event and then the next one—so far, we have hosted more than 40 different events.

All of our events are very diverse because they are initiated by different kids who want to put their passion into action. An example of this is our Thanksgiving Bread Bake (which I started back in second grade, way before starting Kids Helping Kids, and it continues to grow), and this past November we baked and sold more than 1,000 loaves of bread. We used to bake the bread in our kitchen and sell them to friends, family and people at church. However, this past year, ShopRite invited our team into its professional bakery to help us make and wrap the bread in half the time. They even gave us a little pizza party while our bread was cooling. It is so exciting when local businesses offer to help us because they recognize the work we are doing within the community! We have raised more than $20,000 for local kids in need with this one program.

We also host quarterly birthday parties for kids who live in a local Stamford, Connecticut shelter. A shelter isn't normally a place where kids get to celebrate their birthdays, so we wanted to make their birthdays special for them. Our Kids Helping Kids members even make the cupcakes.

With our "Share Your Shoes" project, we have collected more than 16,500 pairs of gently used shoes and sneakers to help people who do not have money to buy them on their own. We give them to the local shelters. The best part is that every December, we create a really cool and realistic shoe store where we get to fit the homeless "customers" who come through. The pop-up shoe store is entirely run by kids! Last year, my mom helped us get a $500 grant so we could buy 500 pairs of socks and give them out with the free shoes.

We have also done work globally, traveling to Nicaragua every August as our big international trip of the year. Ali and Nicole Ambrosecchio, friends of mine and active members of Kids Helping Kids, have family there. They were interested in helping the children over there, especially by giving them the resources to get an education. In 2010, we went there for 10 days to find out how we could help. We have been working with the kids in Nagarote, Nicaragua ever since. We help them build water filtration systems, play with them, tutor them in math and other school subjects and share our friendship with them, in addition to bringing lots of clothes, oral hygiene supplies and other things that will benefit their everyday lives. This year, we are teaching them how to build solar ovens!

We were happy that a big group of kids and older adults from an assisted living facility knitted hats to raise money for the students' education in Nicaragua. To help raise awareness and even more money for the kids, we have had bake sales and also held an "Energizing Education" event, which was a night of fun and friendly exercise-based competitions with prizes and food. And a few years ago, we had an event to increase the importance of clean water in the world. Our "Workout for Wells" event allowed us to build a well in South Sudan in Africa so kids could get clean water and go to school at the same time.

We recently came up with the idea of an ambassadors' program in order to expand the work that we do at Kids Helping Kids. We now have 59 kids serving as Kids Helping Kids spokespersons and appointed contact people at their schools. They enable us to really spread the word and hopefully bring new members into our group. This growing team has allowed us to expand to more schools and to get more great ideas! Our team is now working on our third annual "Launching Libraries" project where we will help rebuild libraries by collecting gently used books. Over the past two years, we have collected and distributed more than 24,000 books! This year (2013) we collected 19,122 books! I could keep going on about what we have created, but I think you get my point: Kids can make an impact in the world in a BIG way. We can shift the world, little by little, and we can do it NOW!

Lexi

PUT YOUR PASSION INTO ACTION!

Lexi is the founder of Kids Helping Kids Connecticut. Start helping in your community by teaming up with Lexi and forming your own Kids Helping Kids chapter at your school. Or you can simply gather together a group of your friends and work on a local charity project. Find more ways to help at KidsHelpingKidsCT.org.

Advocating Through Friendship

by

Danielle Liebl and Kaitlyn Smith

Dear Kaitlyn,

In my short 21 years of life, I have had many struggles and many blessings, but rarely have I been given someone who has helped me turn my struggles into blessings. That someone is you. The friendship we share is so special to me. Having cerebral palsy since birth, I have been bullied numerous times. I was always told of the things I "can't" do instead of the things I "can" do. And I never truly believed that I could have a friend who would see past my disability.

It wasn't until I joined Special Olympics, more than 12 years ago, that I realized how the possibilities were endless for me. Special Olympics has given me many things: it has given me courage, a voice, skills and a place to call home. But one of the most valuable things I learned through our friendship is that just because they call me a Special Olympics athlete does not make me any less valuable than you.

In your eyes, I'm not disabled. I am a human being whom you call a friend. Thank you for being able to laugh with me, cry with me and to develop my leadership skills with me. A friend is not someone who is just there with you, a friend is one who stands by your side, fights for what you believe in and will be your partner in changing the world. Thank you for changing my world.

Love always,
Danielle

Dear Danielle,

I can honestly say that before I met you, I never knew what it truly meant to have a best friend. I have had my fair share of good friends, but I never felt comfortable to be myself. I never felt that I was being everything that I could be. This all changed the minute I got involved with Special Olympics, and the instant I became your friend.

The first time I heard you speak about the struggles and discrimination you faced growing up with cerebral palsy, it made me look at life from a different perspective. It helped me realize how the problems that seemed enormous to me were insignificant when looked at through a different set of eyes. Things that seemed second nature to me were often a huge challenge for people with disabilities. I was leading my life sheltered and selfish before you helped open my eyes.

Every day, you inspire me to be the best person I can be. Through Special Olympics, school work or any other challenge, you are always a friend I can count on to back me up and support me in whatever I need. Thank you for showing me the importance of being unique, being strong and standing up for what you believe in.

Love you always,
Kaitlyn

The summer of 2010 is a summer that will always be remembered by the both of us. It was a summer of growth, new beginnings and cherished memories, but most importantly, it was the summer our lives intersected for the first time. That summer, Special Olympics hosted the 2010 National Youth Activation Summit in Omaha, Nebraska which both of us attended.

Danielle was an intern while Kaitlyn participated as a Unified Partner with her friend Kathleen. We briefly met at the summit when Danielle went up to Kaitlyn's Partner, Kathleen, to wish her a happy birthday. Little did we know that we had each just met a lifelong friend. Later that year, Kaitlyn joined Special Olympics' National Youth Activation Committee, in which Danielle was already a member. At our first meeting in Washington, D.C., we instantly bonded over our uncontrollable laughter, similar sarcasm and sense of humor.

Our friendship was growing, and our friendship meant the world to the both of us. The comfort to be ourselves when we were around each other was proof that we were perfect friends. We never felt compelled to try to impress anyone or be anything we weren't. There was comfort in having conversations about anything, from schoolwork to philosophy.

There was one conversation in particular that has stuck with both of us and has really helped define our friendship. While in Florida attending a Special Olympics marketing and communications meeting, we found ourselves awake at one o'clock in the morning discussing our friendship and the impact it has had. After a lengthy conversation, we came to the realization that not once in our friendship had we ever looked at one another as an "athlete" or a "partner." That simply did not matter.

Over time, we came to realize that the friendship we had wasn't just a normal friendship—it was something much more special. We both had the same ambitions in Special Olympics, similar personalities and we shared a goal to change the world. We were both on the same path, and it didn't take long for us to realize that our friendship would help us support and guide each other in our work for this very special organization.

We realized that our friendship was not one that average youth got to experience very often. It was one that gave us hope on so many levels; not only did it give us hope in our everyday lives, but it also gave us hope for the future. Throughout our friendship, we realized that we wanted nothing more than for all youth to have the friendship that we have—one where friends don't see the limits of each other, but rather where they see each other's full potential.

We wanted to set an example for those around us, and Special Olympics gave us the perfect way to do it. When we first started our advocacy work, we barely realized we were doing it. We did nothing more than make our perfectly normal friendship visible to others.

In the beginning, we didn't realize the impact it was having on others until the staff at Special Olympics brought it to our attention. Before we knew it, we were being asked to talk about our unique friendship to others in the Special Olympics community, and then to the broader community. We took on a new leadership role as we were now being leaders who set an example for a new way of thinking and living. We were the examples of how to live a unified life.

Through our unified friendship that was developed out of Special Olympics, we discovered one of the most powerful ways of activism. Advocacy does not need to be an out-loud verbal expression that you proclaim to a crowd of people. Rather, we discovered that true advocates are the ones who pave a path to a way of life that is often at first unknown or mysterious to others, but ultimately leads to an incredible and fulfilling life. For us, something as simple as our friendship led us to pave this path on which we hope more youth will travel.

Danielle and Kaitlyn

CHERISH YOUR FRIENDS!

Danielle and Kaitlyn are Special Olympics youth leaders. These best friends have proven what a powerful force true friendship can be in changing the world. Cherish the friends you have, be open to new friendships and use the bonds of those relationships to help others in need around you. Please visit SpecialOlympics.org and R-word.org (R-word: Spread the Word to End the Word).

OMG!

by

Carter Ries and Olivia Ries

We have been adopting cheetahs in South Africa since we were five and three years old, respectively. One day, we asked our parents why animals needed to be adopted. Our dad told us that unless there were agencies like the one we had been working with to save cheetahs, there most likely would not be any cheetahs in the wild for *our* kids to see.

Well, that made us really sad and angry! We told our parents that we wanted to save cheetahs for our kids to someday see and enjoy. Dad told us that when we grew up, he and Mom would help us start our own organization to help save endangered species. That wasn't good enough for us, so we kept pestering our parents and asking them when we were going to start our organization, as in, let's do it right now! After a few weeks, Mom and Dad finally gave in and helped us start our own nonprofit, which we called One More Generation (OMG). Our goal with OMG is to help save endangered species for at least one more generation and hopefully beyond. We did not want animals to keep dying and never to be seen again. We set out to learn as much as we could about animals and what was causing them to become endangered, or even worse, extinct.

As we learned more and more, we told our parents we wanted to teach other kids about what was happening so they, too, could get involved and help save animals. We started going to schools and talking to students and their teachers about the importance of getting involved. We even spoke at churches and helped them to develop programs where the whole congregation could help in our mission.

Then in May 2010, about seven months after we started OMG, the Deepwater Horizon oil spill happened in the Gulf of Mexico. We still remember coming home from school and watching CNN and seeing the first pictures of sea turtles and sea birds being pulled out of the ocean, covered in oil and barely alive. It made us very sad all over again.

We asked our parents how we could get involved with helping all those poor animals. Mom and Dad called the four agencies that were responsible for helping to save the animals in the Gulf and asked if we could help them collect badly needed supplies. The answer was, "Yes!"

We spent the next four months going door-to-door to every church, school and Scouting organization in our area and giving presentations about why they needed to help us collect the animal rescue supplies. Then, on Olivia's eighth birthday, we drove 11.5 hours down to the Gulf region where we spent the next five days helping out. We worked with the amazing folks from the Marine Mammal and Sea Turtle Rescue Center, who gladly accepted all our supplies. We even learned how to get oil out (yes, *out*) of a sea turtle. A really smart veterinarian had figured out that if you squirt mayonnaise down a turtle's throat, it would cause it to throw-up and all the oil would come out with it. Pretty cool, huh?

On our last day, a professor who was helping with the animal rescue efforts came up and thanked us for all our hard work. But then she asked what we were doing about the environment. She told us that oil was not the only problem, but that plastic pollution was an even bigger threat to these animals. Did you know that each year more than 100,000 marine mammals and more than one million sea birds die from eating plastic trash?

That's all we had to hear!

We came home and spent the next five months educating ourselves (and our parents) on the issue of plastic pollution. We then decided to get teachers to help us create a program that we could give to schools so they, too, could teach every student about the issue. To educate kids about plastic pollution, we now offer a weeklong program to schools consisting of five individual 45-minute curriculum segments.

This is just one more project, among many, that we have now added to our ever-growing mission to help animals, and we don't plan to stop there. During these past few years, we have learned a lot about not only saving endangered animals, but about the importance of helping all animals in order to insure a healthy planet for more generations to come.

As you learn more about One More Generation, we hope you will always remember that anybody can make a difference. If we can, you can, too!

Olivia and Carter

LOOK TO THE FUTURE!

Carter and Olivia are the founders of One More Generation. Follow this brother and sister's lead and don't just think about today, but also think about how the actions you take now will benefit future generations. Choose a project like preserving the environment or helping out animals so that your children and grandchildren can enjoy them, too. Start looking to the future now at OneMoreGeneration.org.

Legislating Change

by

Carrie Sandstrom

During my junior year of high school, I thought I would be focusing on getting good grades, not tripping frequently in the hallways, and managing to keep a pet goldfish alive. How wrong I was. Instead, I found myself focusing on a much bigger, much more meaningful goal—making the roads safer for teens like myself.

I've considered myself a politician at heart since I first successfully talked my parents into letting me have a later bedtime. Therefore, I was quick to say "yes" when asked by North Dakota's Students Against Destructive Decisions (SADD) coordinator if I would be willing to join a committee of individuals from across the state who were interested in getting a graduated driver's license (GDL) bill passed in the state. I didn't know much about the issue at the time, but I put my name on the list. I can honestly say my life hasn't been the same since.

SADD has always had strong ties to traffic safety. Founded originally as Students Against Driving Drunk, since day one the organization has been dedicated to lowering the number of teen fatalities on the road. As the organization grew, so did its mission. With its new name, SADD now focuses on a larger variety of goals, including traffic safety issues and youth empowerment. For me, the opportunity to work on passing legislation to make North Dakota's roads safer seemed like a perfect marrying of those two goals.

At first, it was intimidating to join in on conference calls with respected members of the community, successful professionals and members of the state legislature. However, I quickly learned that adults respected the youth voice and perspective. I began to see my role on the committee as a spokesperson for all of North Dakota's youth—a role I did not take lightly.

As the beginning of the legislative session drew closer (our state legislature meets every two years for a limited number of days), I fell into a frenzy of emailing, communicating and talking about the importance of reforming North Dakota's driver's license program in order to lessen youth deaths on the roads. But I didn't want to stop there. I connected with other legislators and also began working on a texting and driving ban, as teens and other drivers who text and drive have a significantly higher chance of running into trouble on the road.

After talking about these two bills for months, the start of the legislative session was upon us. I had my testimonies typed, my outfits selected and had practiced introducing myself to the people who had the power to improve the lives of teens throughout the state. But despite my preparation, when I found myself actually standing in front of the Senate and House transportation committees, I was nervous. My legs—thankfully hidden behind a podium—were shaking, my palms were sweating and I was worried I would end up stuttering my way into disgrace. However, as I began to speak, I found the people in front of me were responding in a way I had not thought possible: they were agreeing with me. After the committee sessions were over, many came up and congratulated me on taking a stand, on being brave and on doing something so many teens neglect to do—use their voices.

I testified a total of four nerve-racking times, and by the end, I felt mildly accomplished with what I had done. The hard work of the GDL committee members, the state legislators and community members resulted in the passage of both the graduated driver's license bill and the texting and driving ban. I was ecstatic! I was also blessed to be able to speak at the bill signing and to stand next to the governor as he signed his name to the bill.

Working to pass these bills, I came to realize that it takes the efforts of many individuals to make a difference. I also learned that change can only happen if people are willing to open their minds and their hearts to the possibility of a different reality. Most importantly, though, I experienced the power of the teen voice.

It turns out that in some things, teens actually do know best. SADD has always taught me that if the problem is mine, then the solution lies with me as well. But to see that principle materialize was truly life-changing. Teens have things to say. We live the dangers on the road, we live the peer pressure and, unfortunately, sometimes we live the loss. But we don't have to. We don't have to be condemned to accepting the status quo and we definitely don't have to sit by and passively hope someone else will care.

We teens have voices, passion and the ability to make a difference. So while I may have gone through a few pet goldfish my junior year and tripped occasionally in the hallway, it was worth it because in return, I got so much more.

Carrie

HELP MAKE THE LAWS!

Carrie is a SADD National Student of the Year recipient. As Carrie proved, everyone—including young people like YOU—has a powerful voice. Learn how bills are created and laws are passed, and contact your local government officials, your members of Congress and even the President of the United States to let them all know how you feel about an issue that's important to you. Or, consider running for office yourself someday! Here are some great websites to help you learn more about the political process and how laws are made: WhiteHouse.gov (The White House), Senate.gov (United States Senate), House.gov (The United States House of Representatives) and NGA.org (National Governors Association). To learn more about the important work Carrie and SADD are doing, please visit SADD.org.

The Journey to Equality

by

Giovanna Guarnieri

As a child, I dreamt I would make a difference in the world. I dreamt that I would be a doctor, a president or a teacher. It never fazed me that it might be difficult to reach these goals or that these goals might be unattainable. I thought whatever I decided to be is what I would automatically be. Not until I was older did I learn about the harsh realities of gender discrimination, which many people are still not aware of.

Women were the last group of people to gain suffrage (the right to vote) in the United States, and in some countries they are still treated like property. They have had a long journey to equality, and some women are still on that journey today. Even as a child, I would hear the stereotypical thoughts of some of my young classmates who would say, "Girls cannot do this because . . ."

It always bothered me, but as a child, I thought this was normal and that this was just how things were. Everyone is exposed to certain lessons and experiences in life, good and bad. At such a young age, the children saying those things would have only developed that opinion from their experiences or from something they heard at home. Most likely, one way or another, their parents' views influenced them to think that way. Until people are exposed to the reality of how others are treated, and how much they have to suffer to have certain rights, many people will never fully understand and never be aware of how lucky they are.

In middle school, I did a project on women's suffrage for National History Day. If it were not for this project, I would not have ignited my passion for activism and women's rights. This research taught me how diligently women in the United States have had to work for their rights. To this day, things are still not equal. Needless to say, this project was an eye-opener for me.

With my new passion, I joined a club in seventh grade called School Girls Unite. I went in not knowing a lot, but knowing whatever I could do to help would at least make a difference. My first day in the club, I was assigned to write a summary of Miriam's story to put onto a tri-fold board for our school's Gifted and Talented Enrichment Fair.

Miriam was a 12-year-old girl from Mali, Africa who had to walk many miles every morning for water, return home, do chores, and then walk several more miles to school. After she came home from school, she would have to do more chores and tend to her family. With all this work, it was difficult for her to stay in school. Most girls Miriam's age would end up becoming wives and mothers and would not be able to stay in school.

Miriam's story was one that would come up time after time at School Girls Unite events. It was a moving story that showed a real life example of how girls would be living their lives if they were born in a country with a similar mindset or laws. Our club eventually raised enough money to send 75 girls in Mali to school, and also to educate families on the benefits of keeping their daughters in school and delaying marriage.

Along with helping girls go to school, we worked on getting girls' rights acknowledged in Africa and America. Our School Girls Unite chapter wrote to our county council chairperson, requesting a commemorative day to recognize girls' rights. As a result, Howard County, Maryland became the first county in the country to proclaim the "Day of the Girl." I also helped to plan a celebration that included the state proclamation, which our club wrote and that was signed by the governor, recognizing October 11, 2012 as the Maryland Day of the Girl.

Our purpose was to focus on the unique challenges girls face around the world, and all the opportunities some girls take for granted. We wanted people to realize that girls today have to fight for where they stand. For example, some countries declare that their girls have equal rights, but that isn't true.

As middle school came to an end, I began to think about high school. Many girls in countries such as Mali cannot even imagine going to high school. The sad reality of that made me determined to continue to use my voice, so we focused on girls' rights in this African country. Because of this, we began to work on a game called "Global Equality Now." Global Equality Now was designed like a game show that asked basic gender equality questions and gave an explanation when the answer was given.

We planned to make the game and send it out to many middle and high schools around our county, state and across the country. Our goal was to get people educated, get them involved and get them in the loop. Global Equality Now was our gateway to achieve that goal. The game was a fun way to educate people on girls' rights and raise awareness about the discrimination that millions of girls face because of their gender.

I, along with another student, came to school and edited, re-watched and fine-tuned Global Equality Now every day for about two months. All our hard work and efforts paid off when we saw our final product and were able to start sharing it. You can check out our Global Equality Now game at SchoolGirlsUnite.org/learn.

With the help of teachers from my middle school and high school, I started a chapter of School Girls Unite at my high school, of which I can proudly say I am co-president. It is amazing to know that I, as a teenager, am part of a team of people committed to making a difference in the world.

There are those who may think all of this is not worth it. I believe there is no statement that could be considered more false. I believe our group can make a difference. We already have! And so can anyone else, no matter their age or where they live.

To make a difference, all you have to do is believe in yourself and believe in fairness, equality and justice!

Giovanna

YOU ARE EQUAL!

Giovanna is the co-president of the School Girls Unite chapter at her school. No matter where you live or what your circumstances are, know that you deserve to be an equal member of society! That is your right as a human being. Stand up for that right and fight for that right for both yourself and others around the world. Learn more at SchoolGirlsUnite.org, YouthActivismProject.org and DayOfTheGirl.org.

The Power of "We"

by

Mariah Smiley

Have you ever felt a stirring deep inside, a desire to step out and do something great, yet were unsure of where to start? I have, and I remember the day I found my starting point—the day that I realized my passion—a day that would define the rest of my life.

My parents came home from a charity fundraising gala and told me a stunning fact: one child dies every 15 seconds from a lack of clean water. This floored me and I absolutely couldn't believe it! My heart got a feeling that I cannot even begin to describe as I talked with my parents more about this global water crisis.

They told me so many sad statistics, which were a direct result of people not having access to clean water. But I also learned there was hope. For example, $1 provides clean water to one person for one year. I was like, "WOW . . . only $1 can save a life?"

That night, I decided to take a stand and raise money to provide clean water to the needy. Although I was only 14 years old, I made a decision to do something because surely I could save or raise $100 or $200 or more. It seemed very possible that I could make a real impact.

To start, I created a charity called Drops of Love. I was so excited about my new charity that I couldn't sleep that first night. Soon, with a little help, I coded a basic website on my laptop, hand-drew a logo and emailed a local nonprofit to learn more and to create a plan moving forward. Over the last three years, these simple acts have grown into what is now the full-fledged Drops of Love organization.

Of course, I haven't done this all by myself. I was blessed to have met people who understood my passion and my heartfelt desire to help. Many people and organizations patiently worked with me and walked beside me to teach me valuable lifelong lessons. I learned a lot about people and their willingness to go the extra mile to help others reach their dreams.

One of my first fundraisers was talking in front of my entire high school, educating the students and faculty about the water crisis and challenging them to help. I was so nervous, but everyone was eager to help, and together we raised more than $1,000 that day. This gave me the confidence to do more, and over the next three years, through a variety of fundraisers, Drops of Love raised more than $20,000 and funded four new wells!

In 2011, my family traveled to El Salvador to drill a well that was funded by Drops of Love. I was forever changed by that trip and the people we worked with and met during that week. The parents and children of our sponsored village were so excited to see the well team and watched us work each day.

My Spanish isn't very good, but I tried to explain to the children what was happening anyway. I said, "No mas mal agua." That translated to, "No more bad water." They looked at me with dumbfounded stares, and I was worried that I had made a Spanish language blunder. But when they saw the crystal clear water flowing out of that well pump, I realized my Spanish was fine. They were just amazed that this could be true, that they would have fresh water. There were giggles, tears, hugs, prayers and many thanks shared all around.

I watched as they tasted this clean water, which is something that they had been living without for a very long time, and smiled as they happily washed their feet. That moment made everything real—I realized there were faces behind all those horrific statistics and they were children just like me—children who loved to laugh and play and even go to school. The only difference between us was where we were born. It confirmed my mission that together we can save lives.

Recently, I was able to realize another dream. Generous volunteers helped Drops of Love become an official nonprofit organization. I never thought that at age 17, I would need to know about corporate structures, taxes and board meetings, but I am learning about these and many other business issues.

Drops of Love now has a talented volunteer board of directors, who support the vision of Drops of Love and spend countless hours preparing the way for Drops of Love to grow in new directions. In addition to local fundraisers, Drops of Love is now working to establish corporate relationships and sponsorships.

Also, we are launching a very exciting program within schools. Drops of Love is creating local school chapters to empower students to help raise awareness of the water crisis and to save lives. Each chapter will be provided with print materials and all the support needed to host fundraisers and organize sponsorships for wells. Drops of Love wants to assist teens who have the desire to make a difference and will help every step of the way.

Drops of Love has gotten a lot of great visibility lately. Last year alone, we were highlighted in a number of newspapers and magazines, as well as invited to speak to a variety of organizations. Raising awareness of the global water crisis and how everyone can help is the example I wish to live through Drops of Love.

Drops of Love was founded by a teen who knew inside her heart the power of teens and how all teens could make a difference. We—the teenagers of the world—are the future and must learn from the selfless adults who are paving the way.

People are sometimes surprised by my story. But it is not about the power of "me," it is about the power of "we." I want to make sure everyone remembers that a small sacrifice can make a big difference!

Mariah

TURN YOUR "ME" INTO "WE"!

Mariah is the founder of Drops of Love. One of the main messages in her story is that you are not alone in the world, no matter who you are or what your interests and talents may be. Find other people who share your interests in making the world a better place and join together with them. Turn your "me" into a productive and charitable "WE." Please visit DropsOfLove.org.

CHAPTER FOUR

 The Adventure Seekers

From Africa's tallest mountain to the high seas, from faraway exotic jungles to exciting journeys close to home, there are no limits for those who seek to change the world for the better.

Kilimanjaro for a Cause!

by

Tyler Armstrong

When I was only eight and a half years old, I climbed to the top of Mount Kilimanjaro in Tanzania, Africa, and became the second youngest person to ever stand on top.

The climb took place in July 2012, the summer before I started third grade. Mount Kilimanjaro is 19,341 feet high and the tallest mountain in Africa. It is also the tallest freestanding mountain in the world. It took my dad and me eight days to climb the whole mountain. Six days up and two days down. This is the story of how I did it.

I climb mountains for my friends who have Duchenne. Duchenne is a muscular disease that only affects boys. They are usually diagnosed at the age of five, and as they quickly lose muscle mass in their legs, they become weak and cannot walk. I was able to raise more than $11,000 to donate to an organization called CureDuchenne to help fund research to try to save my friends' lives someday. I also did a lot of television shows to help raise awareness about Duchenne.

When I got to Tanzania with my dad, I met another boy who had Duchenne. This meant a lot to me. I also met a local governor and the newspaper came to talk to me and wish me luck on my climb. At the government office on the mountain, there is a sign posted that says no kids under 10 years old are allowed on the mountain. But the government of

Tanzania gave me a special permit because I had already set a record for climbing Mount Whitney (the highest summit in the contiguous United States). After we got the permit to climb Mount Kilimanjaro, we drove to the beginning of the trail, but the road was muddy. Our car almost tipped over. It was crazy.

It was surprising how many people were going on the climb with my dad and me. The group included my dad's friend, a dad of a friend of mine who has Duchenne and two of his friends, a doctor to keep me safe, and my sponsor—who was able to get the special climbing permit for me—and her friend, too. What was incredible was that for us nine climbers, we had a support crew of 25 locals from Tanzania. There was one guide especially for me. For the rest of the group, there were another three guides and support crew who carried the gear and set up camp. It was amazing to have so many people there to help me get to the top.

On the first day of our climb, it was thundering and raining and there were many mud streams. The trail was very slippery. We saw monkeys. We did not get to camp until after dark. I was cold and muddy, but we had to get clean before we could go into our tents. On the second day, we started climbing higher, up and out of the rainforest. It started sprinkling. I had soup for lunch. We climbed to the top of the ridge and there was another ridge. By the time we got to camp, there were no more trees, but only small bushes.

The third day, my legs started hurting. The doctor said I had a fever. I toughed it out and drank a box of juice so I could keep hiking. With another hour to go, my dad made a CureDuchenne sign in the sand. He wanted to keep me motivated, to remind me I was climbing to the top of Mount Kilimanjaro to raise money to cure Duchenne. When we finally got to camp, the Tanzanian cooks made a special drink with lemon and ginger to make my stomach, which had been bothering me, feel better.

The fourth day, I started hiking at 8:30 A.M. and hiked for hours before I had an awesome lunch of fried chicken and cucumber soup! Then we kept climbing and I got higher than I ever did before. We climbed beyond 14,505 feet, which is the same height as Mount Whitney. Some of my dad's friends climbed a really big rock, but my dad wouldn't let me because he was afraid that if I got hurt, I wouldn't make it to the top of Mount Kilimanjaro. Then we went down to camp. Some other hikers recognized me from TV and wanted to take pictures with me.

On day five, I climbed a cliff. It was about 2,000 feet and it took me an hour and a half to climb it. It was like rock climbing with my hands. The doctor in our group saved one of the porter's bags from falling off the cliff. I hiked for another two hours and I helped to set up camp and had dinner and slept.

On day six, I walked up another 2,000 feet. It took us a couple of hours and we then had to walk up another cliff. My dad told me to eat some M&Ms to give me energy. That night I ate chicken fingers and fries. And I had reached a new height at 15,300 feet! There were a lot of other climbers at this base camp. Other trails coming up the mountain all led here.

On summit day, we started hiking at midnight. It was very dark and very cold—only about eight degrees Fahrenheit. It was so cold that our drinking water kept freezing. I have never seen so many stars in the sky. It seemed like there were millions.

After the sun came up, I felt a little warmer. That's when I saw the top of Mount Kilimanjaro! Did you know that Mount Kilimanjaro is an old volcano? At the top, I could look down into the crater where lava used to be 200,000 years ago. It is all ice now. I was super excited to get to the top and be the second youngest person to ever do so!

I took pictures with the Mount Kilimanjaro summit sign to show I had reached the top, and with some things my friends gave me to take to the top. My friend Wil, who has Duchenne, gave me his cross to keep me safe on the mountain, so I took pictures with Wil's cross to show him that a part of him also made it to the top of Mount Kilimanjaro. My friend Brianna from school also gave me a bracelet as a symbol to keep me safe.

At the top, I looked down and the clouds looked like one big humongous pillow. I saw huge glaciers and they were super white. It felt really cool and I was amazed because I learned that in 20 years, all the glaciers on Mount Kilimanjaro will be gone. The guides told me that five years earlier, we wouldn't have been able to sleep at the last camp because the area would have been covered in ice. But when I was there, the ice sheet that was once at the camp had melted away. The ice now started much higher up the mountain.

Coming down from the top of Kilimanjaro was really fun because we ran down the rocks, which are called "scree." It was like we were skiing on small rocks and sand. We went so fast that my dad and the doctor could not keep up with us. The porters were all celebrating my accomplishment and they carried me on their shoulders and sang an African mountain song in Swahili. Then they made me a cake on the mountain! It was awesome!

When we finally got to the bottom, my mom and little brother, Dylan, were waiting for me. I went and signed the logbook at the government office at the trail's end and got a certificate showing I made it to the top of Mount Kilimanjaro.

It was really fun that I made it to the top for my friends with Duchenne—I raised more than $11,000 for them! What I learned is that the more I climb, the more money I can get for the boys and help find a cure for them. I was excited that my hike made so many people want to help these boys and me. During the climb to the top, my legs got really tired and it felt like they did not want to work. It made me realize what kids with Duchenne must feel like because the muscles in their legs don't work and every year older the boys get, it becomes harder and harder for them to walk.

This climb up Mount Kilimanjaro taught me that raising money is not easy and you have to work hard to help others. I also learned that when climbing gets really hard in really high altitudes, just like in other aspects of life, I have to keep going and must not give up.

Tyler

AIM FOR THE TOP!

Tyler is a mountain climber and advocate for CureDuchenne. Whether you're climbing the world's highest mountain for a great cause or facing everyday challenges, follow Tyler's example and keep moving onward and upward until you reach your goal. Take the first step of your climb to help yourself and others by checking out TopWithTyler.com and CureDuchenne.org.

Living on the Wild Side

by

Janine Licare

All children dream of living at the zoo: getting to play with monkeys, sloths, anteaters, porcupines and wild birds every day. For me, that was just my ordinary childhood.

When I was four years old, I moved from the suburbs of Connecticut to the rainforests of Manuel Antonio, Costa Rica, Central America. No longer would I see street signs and cars outside my window, or snow at wintertime, but rather monkeys in my backyard and rain six months out of the year. I was living in the jungle.

My new hometown was very rural. We didn't have malls, movie theatres, playgrounds or even streetlights, so I had to find other ways to entertain myself. Needless to say, I grew quite interested in the rainforest and the animals that lived in it, and made studying it my new hobby. Over the years I started to notice how the trees around me became fewer and fewer as the rainforest slowly began to disappear. Suddenly, Manuel Antonio wasn't as rural as it had once been, but was now being flooded with hotels and restaurants. And all the land that was being developed needed to come from somewhere.

By this time, I was nine years old. My best friend and I decided to start raising money to save the rainforest. We started making arts and crafts and selling our creations. After a few weeks of hard work, we had raised

$80. To congratulate us on our efforts, my mom decided to match the money, so we had $160 to start saving the rainforest.

We had heard of an organization in northern Costa Rica that accepted donations to purchase acres of rainforest to be protected. We donated our money to this organization and were very excited about the land we had saved. A few months later, we went on a road trip to northern Costa Rica to visit the organization. When we got there, they told us that they were very sorry, but they did not know what they had done with our donation, whether it had gone to pay for someone's salary, to pay for administrative operations or something else. We felt cheated!

We decided to no longer donate money to other organizations, but to create our own organization so we would always know where our money was going. This is a principle we hold to this day: Anyone who donates to our nonprofit Kids Saving the Rainforest will get to decide exactly where their money will go. They get to choose whether they want their donation to go to our animal sanctuary, Adopt a Rainforest Tree program, the Monkey Bridge project or any of our many other projects.

After that fateful road trip, we really stepped it up a notch as far as making our arts and crafts. Now that we were our own organization, we needed to start raising more money to fund our own projects. We received help from other children in the neighborhood and our dream started to grow. It was when we got our own website that Kids Saving the Rainforest really took off. We became internationally acclaimed, and as more and more people heard about the organization, we gained more members dedicated to helping us with our mission.

As we grew as an organization, we were able to fund our own projects, including an animal rehabilitation center, a reforestation project, a sister program and others. To date, we have rehabilitated and released more than 500 wild animals, gained more than 5,000 members worldwide and have planted more than 10,000 trees in Costa Rica.

That is how, from the suburbs of Connecticut to the jungles of Costa Rica, saving the rainforest became my new hobby and mission. There were no malls for me to go to or movies for me to see, but I got to spend my childhood playing with monkeys, babysitting sloths and planting trees instead.

Janine

GO WILD FOR A GOOD CAUSE!

Janine is the co-founder of Kids Saving the Rainforest. You never know where your efforts to help the planet are going to lead you—maybe even to a jungle in faraway Costa Rica. No matter the cause, turn it into a fun adventure! You can join Janine's safari to save the planet's wild side by visiting KidsSavingTheRainforest.org.

The Big Sleep Out

by

Peter Larson

In 1996, Bob Fisher, a local shoe repairman from Wayzata, Minnesota decided that he wanted to raise money for a local nonprofit group called Interfaith Outreach and Community Partners (IOCP) to help fight homelessness. He came up with the idea of sleeping outside in the harsh winters and not coming back inside until he was able to reach his goal. It started out as a small event, but over the years it grew and other groups started to sleep out, too.

One of these groups was my Cub Scout pack. When Bob came and talked to us the night of our Cub Scout meeting, he began by telling us about why what he was doing was so important. He explained that the money he raised was used to help prevent families in our community from becoming homeless. These were families where someone had lost a job, had a medical problem or had experienced some other unforeseen event that resulted in the family not having enough money to pay their rent or mortgage.

Bob also told us about children and families in need who probably lived in our own neighborhoods. Then he told us that for every $500 raised, IOCP could prevent a family from becoming homeless. When I heard that number, it just clicked. It was as if someone had told me that this is what I should do, that I could help another family. So that night, I decided I would set a goal for myself and raise money to help IOCP.

That first year and for the next three years, I slept out one night of what was by then officially called The Sleep Out. Each year, I was able to raise more money than the year before. I raised money by speaking to the people in my church and by going door-to-door, talking to neighbors. I told them about homelessness in our community and that if they donated to my Sleep Out efforts, together we could help those families. I think people were surprised to find out that so many people in our community—an affluent suburb of Minneapolis—were in danger of becoming homeless.

Then in the fifth grade, I decided I wanted to do more.

I knew I needed to help more families, so I asked my parents if I could sleep out for the entire event. When I first asked my parents, they were hesitant since it could get so cold out, but after some convincing, they agreed. So with my parents' support, I made a commitment to Bob Fisher and IOCP to sleep out from November 13 to December 24.

My dad and I went to a local appliance store and got an empty refrigerator box, and we put it in our backyard. All I had in that cardboard box was a sleeping mat, my down sleeping bag, my pillow and a light so that I could read before I went to sleep. Every night for six weeks, I would crawl into my cold sleeping bag and snuggle in to get warm.

The hardest part of sleeping outside in the winter wasn't going out to the box that would be my only shelter at night, but getting up in the morning. I was warm in my cardboard shelter, and walking across the snow to get inside my warm house was hard. But it was worth it: that first year, I raised more than $2,000 and kept four families from becoming homeless.

Jill Kohler from IOCP heard about my commitment and became my mentor. Working with Jill, I learned more about what it's like to be homeless. I met with social workers, and I toured homes that were built for affordability. Through IOCP, I had the opportunity to speak to local media, church groups, Boy Scout troops and elementary school students about IOCP and the realities of homelessness in our community.

I'm lucky to live in a community where people care so much, and because of the interviews I did with the local media, donations started coming in from across the state. When I was in eighth grade, two girls from our high school asked if they could interview me and also sleep outside with me for one night. It was December when they came and it was cold out; it is Minnesota, after all. They showed the video at school and the student body was so inspired by it that in one week, they raised $1,000 for me.

There were also a number of elementary schools in our school district that helped raise money for The Sleep Out. One second grade class heard about me and named me one of their heroes. Their teacher asked if I would talk to the class, which I agreed to do. They had me sit in a rocking chair and the kids sat around me and asked all sorts of questions. I think they were surprised that I started sleeping out when I was in first grade. What I told them was that anyone can make a difference in someone's life, no matter how young or old you are.

Families who are in jeopardy of losing their homes are often invisible. You can't tell just by looking at someone if they're on the verge of becoming homeless. Sometimes when I was in school, I'd wonder if one of the kids in my class was on the verge of becoming homeless.

Typically when you volunteer, you can see the person you're helping, but I had never met anyone whom I had helped until I was in the 10th grade. Jill Kohler called and said she had a family she wanted me to meet—a mom and her three daughters. They were just like my family, but they just needed a little help. The mom told me that she was surprised to find out that someone my age had raised the money to help them. She said that someday they wanted to be able help someone like I had helped them. It was very humbling to meet a family I had helped and to have them express so much gratitude for what I had done.

Because I was headed off to college, 2011 was my 12th and final year of sleeping out and raising money for IOCP. I've slept out more than 340 nights and in temperatures as low as -20 degrees Fahrenheit. There were nights when I was afraid my hair might freeze. But I always slept out, no matter what the conditions were.

Over the years, I have raised more than $534,200 and IOCP has used that money to build safe and affordable housing in addition to giving financial assistance to countless families. Every year there is a kickoff for The Sleep Out and each year a growing number of groups participates in the event. This included two little girls who wanted to carry on for me since I was going to college. Bob inspired me, and now I've inspired someone, too. That's a great feeling!

We're all called to help, whether we're five or we're 50. It just depends on whether we're listening. Are you listening?

Peter (above) in 2006
and today (right)

CAMPOUT TO HELP OUT!

Peter is an advocate for Interfaith Outreach and Community Partners' The Sleep Out. This is a great example of taking a fun activity—camping out—and turning it into a mission to help the homeless and others. Ask yourself: *What do I really love to do? How can I use that interest or activity to help others?* You can join The Sleep Out at IOCP.org.

The Sea Olympics

by

Nate Neff

During the spring of my junior year at the University of Pittsburgh at Bradford, I attended a study-abroad program called Semester at Sea. At the time, I was a sports medicine/pre-physical therapy major. Saying that I was excited would be an understatement, considering the fact that I had started my original planning and preparing for the program during the fall of my freshman year.

I had some major goals I wanted to achieve during this voyage of a lifetime. Goals such as, 1) fully immersing myself in the cultures that I would experience; 2) making great friends from all over the United States and the world; 3) removing myself from my comfort zone as much as possible; 4) growing mentally and spiritually as a person; 5) developing a greater understanding of the world as a whole; and, of course, 6) helping out the countries I visited through service and donations.

The other students and I traveled on a small cruise ship to 11 different countries during the process of circumnavigating the globe. The trip lasted 105 days and while sailing, we all took 12 college credits worth of classes. While we were in port, we were free to spend our time exploring and traveling. The voyage started in the Bahamas, and then we sailed to Dominica, Brazil, Ghana, South Africa, Mauritius, India, Singapore, Vietnam, China, Japan and Hawaii before ending in San Diego.

Luckily, I had already made an awesome group of friends by the time we arrived in Brazil. My new friend Taylor from West Virginia University (Yes, I go to the University of Pittsburgh and made a great friend from WVU! What are the odds?) and I had plans to buy certain goods in every country we ported in, and then take those goods to the next country and donate them there. However, because of the fact that we both had extremely low spending budgets compared with the majority of others making up the shipboard community, we realized we would not be able to do what we initially planned.

We didn't let our low budgets stop us. We came up with a new idea to help provide items to those in need. To motivate the shipboard community to assist us in donating, we received permission from our leader to create an event called the Sea Olympics. All of the students were divided into teams named after seas, such as the Caribbean, Baltic and Yellow, depending on where their cabins were located on the ship. Then on the day of the Sea Olympics, all the seas competed against each other in friendly games and competitions like volleyball, synchronized swimming and tug-of-war.

Taylor and I received permission to make our donation drive one of the events of the Sea Olympics and we called it "Charity@Sea." We then created a point system in which certain donations were worth a specific amount of points, such as a book being ten points, pencils/pens being one point each and clothing items ranging in points. The team with the most points totaled from their amount of donations would receive first-place points toward their overall efforts in the Sea Olympics. There were also second and third place points.

By advertising with signs throughout the ship and announcing our idea at a pre-port meeting—these meetings were mandatory for the whole shipboard community—our donation drive turned out to be a great success. The resident director of each team received a large box for the donations to be placed in and everyone could then donate whatever they had. Seeing the majority of the 11 boxes overflowing on the day of the Sea Olympics was a great feeling, especially since we were all confined to a small ship in which each person had only a couple of suitcases worth of belongings to choose from for donations. Each donation box was displayed in a hallway on the ship and I examined them all with a smile on my face, knowing that people in need would be grateful to receive them. With the help of a few friends, we determined which team was the winner of the donation drive.

After all of the donations were separated into categories like books, school supplies, toys and clothes, we had to decide where the materials would be donated. With the help of the resident director, Moises, who led the community service club on the ship, we were able to distribute the donations in an organized manner. Moises played a very key role in helping Charity@Sea become a success. It could not have happened without his assistance.

Some of the donations went to impoverished areas in Cape Town, South Africa, and some went to underprivileged places in a city in southwest India. However, the majority of the items were given to a school in Ho Chi Minh City in southern Vietnam. Another resident director from the ship had a friend who was working at the school in Vietnam and he came to the port where our ship docked with a fellow co-worker. They collected the three boxes of donations to personally take back to the school. The excitement they displayed from receiving the materials definitely made the hard work we all put into Charity@Sea worth it.

Studying abroad with Semester at Sea and starting Charity@Sea during the voyage was an amazing and gratifying experience. My goals that I made before the semester were more than fulfilled. When I stepped off the ship back onto United States' soil, I was a different and better person compared with when I began the voyage. That trip opened my doors to the world, helping me to put life's endeavors into a new perspective.

One of the greatest lessons I learned is that from the big cities of Ho Chi Minh, Hong Kong and Tokyo to the small villages in Ghana and the Amazon rainforest, to way back at the University of Pittsburgh at Bradford in Pennsylvania, everyone has the same general types of problems. We are all one small part of the same world. Even though we all speak different languages, we still all smile and laugh the same way.

All the hard work and dedication that Moises, Taylor and myself (along with the rest of the community service club on the ship) put into Charity@Sea and simply helping others was completely worth it. I was amazingly blessed to have such an experience of a lifetime and to share it with so many awesome people along the way. It's difficult to change the world by yourself. However, if we all take small steps toward doing so, we can still make a huge difference in other people's lives and positively affect the lives of those around us.

I have now adopted the new everyday saying of "Do whatever is more awesome." When I ask myself, "What will I do to make the most out of today?" the answer needs to always be, "I'm going to do whatever is more awesome!"

Exploring the world while providing service and helping others was definitely "more awesome."

Nate

SET SAIL WITH YOUR IMAGINATION!

Nate is the co-founder of Charity@Sea, a one-time project he initiated while participating in the Semester at Sea program. Even in the middle of the vast ocean, or in your own classroom at school, a little creativity and enthusiasm can help you set sail to touch the four corners of the globe with a good cause! Set sail with your imagination by visiting SemesterAtSea.org.

You Can Be Greater Than You Know How to Be

by

Talia Y. Leman

When Hurricane Katrina hit the Gulf Coast in 2005, I had a plan. I made the decision that with Halloween around the corner, I was going to take advantage of that captive audience and trick-or-treat for coins instead of candy. I was then going to give my money to hurricane relief organizations. It seemed a reasonable course of action for a 10 year old.

I called my business "T.L.C.," an acronym which stood for "Trick-or-Treat for the Levee Catastrophe." That is, except when it didn't. Sometimes it stood for "Trick-or-Treat for Loose Change." And sometimes is stood for "Trick-or-Treat for Loads of Cash." I took a flexible approach to branding. I also determined that I would be the CEO of this effort, a title I took to mean "chief executive optimist." Dutiful to my title, I set an early goal of raising $1 million.

By all accounts, things were coming along. I had a nice big trick-or-treat bag and I chose a neighborhood where the houses were really (really) close together. Then my six-year-old brother got wind of what I was up to. He came up to me, clearly very upset, and said, "I am opposed to what you are doing. I'd rather trick-or-treat for pirate relief!" Those were his exact words.

I didn't know what to do with that; it was very unexpected. But I decided to make room for it anyway by offering him a title, too. He became my official CON, or chief operating nemesis. We even put him on our website in his favorite Darth Vader costume, and he was thrilled.

And then something happened that turned my life around forever. Producers at the *TODAY Show* came across our website, saw my brother's photo and invited us to appear on their program. It was CEO vs. CON in front of a national audience, where we told the world about our little trick-or-treat project.

One day later, I was fielding donation reports from kids all over the United States whom we inspired to join their efforts with ours. I tracked their donations on a map with pushpins. One week later, a local grocery chain agreed to print 8.5 million trick-or-treat bags to be given out with my message on them in 226 stores in 13 states. Our governor held a press conference and UNICEF invited me to do media spots on CNN and NPR.

When it came time to draw our efforts to a close, I knew we had raised a considerable amount, but it was not my original goal of $1 million. It wasn't even half a million. No . . . it was $10 million dollars for the survivors of Hurricane Katrina! It's a fact that kids from across the U.S. ranked in their giving power with the top five U.S. corporate donors to Katrina—right up there with Walmart, Exxon Mobil and Amoco Corporation.

Through all of this, I became a witness to a greatness in others that I never could have foreseen—a success I never could have planned. It just happened, which is a scary realization.

If greatness often happens by accident, or by surprise, or if it's not a carefully orchestrated sequence of events, how can we happen upon it? How can we do something greater than we know how to do and become something greater than we know how to be?

I wasn't sure.

But what I was sure of was that someone had to harness that youth power for other disasters the world would face. So I started an organization called RandomKid, which is a unique nonprofit that leverages the power of youth to solve real problems in the world. We provide all the tools and resources young people need to power up their ideas. I figured if we could raise $10 million for hurricane relief, we could do anything!

Today, RandomKid has unified the efforts of 12 million youth from 20 countries. And for every dollar we invest in a youth's idea, these young people turn it around into a 150-percent to 1,000-percent return for their cause. Working with us at RandomKid, young people have now placed safe water wells on four continents, built and refurbished schools both overseas and on our Gulf Coast, provided wind energy to bring water to once-parched gardens and so much more.

Despite all that success, do you know the most common question people ask me? It's why I decided to call my organization RandomKid. It turns out to be a very important question. I tell them, quite simply, it's because I am a random kid. I tell them it's because if I see myself as anything more than a random kid then how will those I seek to empower see the potential that they have? I also tell them it's because when we believe in the power we each have, we have the greatest power of all.

But the greatest message of my journey lies in the realization that RandomKid's success did not happen because of my ambitious Katrina goals or my lofty title of chief executive optimist. RandomKid's success happened because of . . . did you catch it? RandomKid's success happened because I made room for my brother—Darth Vader! It was the one step I took that seemed to have nothing to do with my success and it became the very thing that made me successful.

So, then, how can we do something greater than we know how to do and become something greater than we know how to be, when it is often serendipity that gets us there?

I now know the answer.

Greatness happens when we make room for the plan we didn't have—when we are free enough and brave enough to take a step sideways to a place where unexpected things might happen. And do you know why that is? Because the great miracles of life, by definition, can only appear in those unexpected places.

Greatness happens by making room for passions that don't make sense, for playfulness that has no purpose, for ideas that are not your own, for people who are not like you, for a path you didn't define, for a dream you were afraid to dream, for a future you didn't imagine.

By making room for the unexpected, you can sometimes follow your heart to a larger destiny, be captured by a grander idea, realize a power you never knew, choose a path that raises you higher, dream that impossible dream, believe yourself into a new way of being and create a future defined by miracles and marked with a greatness you never thought possible.

The answer is that we don't always have to know the how. We can just head in the direction of the unexplainable kismet that pulls us forward, and we will get there.

Talia

MAKE ROOM FOR THE UNEXPECTED!

Talia is the founder of RandomKid. Life is full of twists and turns, with surprises around every corner. When you open your mind to the possibilities and opportunities waiting for you in those places, great things will happen, just like they did for Talia. See what happens when you embrace the unexpected at RandomKid.org.

CHAPTER FIVE

 Tasty Activism

By harnessing the power of
healthy foods and lifestyles,
we nourish ourselves,
each other and the planet
—one bite at a time.

The Rainbow Salad

by

Kirsten Gerbatsch

On an autumn day just around lunchtime at Northport Public School in Michigan, I stood behind the kitchen service counter beside Janis and Brenda. I donned a hairnet to hold back my long hair and wrapped a black apron around my waist. A huge bowl of salad was on the counter in front of me, filled with a collage of color—rich red beets, bright yellow peppers, dark baby greens, bold orange tomatoes and deep purple cabbage. Beside the salad were a bunch of white, orange and purple carrots and a bowl of Sun Gold tomatoes.

As students lined up at one end of the counter to receive a slice of pizza, some fruit and a carton of milk, they noticed me at the far end, and their eyes grew wide with excitement. Then they saw the bunch of carrots and the tomato bowl.

"Hey! Those are our carrots! And our tomatoes! We picked those today!" the second graders yelled as they urgently slid their trays down the line to meet me.

"Would you like to try some Rainbow Salad?" I asked. "It's got veggies from our school garden in it."

"Yes, please!" each student chimed.

I served up one generous portion of Rainbow Salad after another. Even though pizza and chocolate milk already owned real estate on the young students' trays, I didn't lose my momentum. Each student that afternoon ate a great big portion of fresh vegetables—and they enjoyed it, too. The bowl of tomatoes and the entire bunch of carrots vanished as children recognized their school-grown carrots and Sun Golds.

One boy asked sheepishly if he could also have a whole carrot, in addition to the Rainbow Salad.

"Well, of course!" I said. I then let him choose a small purple carrot with the stem and leaves still attached.

Every child following also wanted a whole carrot and took great care to choose the carrot that he or she had "definitely" harvested. I watched in amazement as small hands grabbed at the carrots and proudly placed one on their trays. What a sight to see: carrot tops flopping off over the edge of plastic lunch trays as kids skipped off to the cafeteria.

So you might ask, how did I come to find myself in a hairnet and apron, serving up vegetables to elementary school kids? Well, I had begun my first year of service in northwest Lower Michigan with a new national program called FoodCorps, in partnership with the Michigan Land Use Institute.

FoodCorps is a nationwide team of leaders that connects kids to real food and helps them grow up healthy. As one of the first 50 service members in 2011 and as one of the 80 to embark on a second year of service, I partner with teachers, local farmers, food service professionals and volunteers to teach kids about what healthy food is and where it comes from. We also build and tend school gardens and bring high-quality local food into public school cafeterias.

As a second-year FoodCorps service member, I suppose I never really considered myself an activist, per se. I see myself as many things: I am a teacher, a mentor, a gardener, a chef, an artist, a community organizer, a nutritionist and a role model. So, when given the opportunity to share my story, I wondered about a few things. *Am I an activist? A protestor? A zealot? A radical?* At first glance, I thought, *Not really.* But then I realized, *Whoa! I am an activist in every sense of the word.*

I am an activist for healthy school lunches and for the girls and boys who eat them. I protest the cynical, defeating notion that kids don't like vegetables or nutritious food choices, and I bust that myth wide open every day. I am a zealous gardener, and I share this love with my students so that they, too, can learn the satisfaction and pride in growing food and taking care of the land. I am indeed a radical because I think that healthy food is cool and totally normal. I am trying to transform the school food environment in small ways that may have a huge impact on the rest of these children's lives.

The ease and success of the Rainbow Salad lunchroom tasting was not always so at Northport Public School. The food service staff has always been supportive and excited about serving healthy options and sourcing from local farmers, yet they found that the fruits and vegetables placed on the kids' trays usually ended up in the trash. It was disheartening and a waste of time, money and food.

The story of how these students have come to know and love new vegetables started in the school garden, long before fresh carrots and to-matoes arrived on the lunch line. During the spring, I coordinated with the food service staff and teachers to create a school garden from which we could harvest food to serve at lunch and to use as a hands-on education space. Elementary school students helped to grow vegetables and herbs in the garden and they were proud of their plants.

On the morning of our special Rainbow Salad service, the second grade class came out to the garden for the last fall harvest. Together, we pulled carrots of all shapes and sizes from the ground and plucked little tomatoes off the massive, tangled plants. Only a percentage of the produce made it back inside with us to be washed, though. Those children ate the carrots straight out of the ground and the tomatoes right off the vine. And kids who had been scared to get their hands dirty in the garden last spring were now digging in the soil to pull up carrots. It was an incredible transformation.

In addition to the garden produce we harvested, Janis, the food service director at Northport Public School, had purchased vegetables like bell pep-pers, lettuce, cabbage and beets from local county farmers. Janis and I chopped and tossed all the vegetables together and dressed the salad very lightly with some honey balsamic dressing. And then we crossed our fingers!

Janis had agreed to try the Rainbow Salad, but she was nervous it would be a total flop. "The kids just don't eat vegetables," she said repeatedly.

That day, Janis' concern was, to her pleasant surprise, met with an overwhelming amount of brand new exuberant salad eaters who said things like:

"I didn't think I would like this salad, but my carrots are in it so it's really yummy."

"Check out how many colors I have! My salad is the best!"

"These greens are actually good!"

The transformation in the lunchroom and in these children's lives began right there.

The kids might not know it, but I am their biggest fan. I am an activist for them. I am rooting for them every step of the way that they might grow up healthy, able and happy. I am also the lunch ladies' biggest fan because I know they have a hard job. I'm there to support them in what they do best and to show them that we don't have to throw our hands up in the air and give up on our kids' ability to appreciate good food.

We can't afford to give up. As a FoodCorps service member, I am standing up for the health of the next generation and I am standing strong.

And I must say, I am serving up some tasty activism.

Kirsten

PLAY IN THE DIRT!

Kirsten is a FoodCorps service member who helped her students discover just how fun and tasty playing in the dirt can be! Plus, they discovered how delicious fresh vegetables are. Try making your own Rainbow Salad at home with different colored vegetables from a garden, a local farmers' market or the grocery store. And find out how you can start a garden at your school or in your own backyard at FoodCorps.org.

Birke on the Farm

by

Birke Baehr

When I was eight years old, I was looking over my mom's shoulder early one morning while she was logging into her email. On her home page, I noticed an interesting headline that stuck out like a sore thumb: "Mercury Found in High Fructose Corn Syrup." I had learned about mercury in third grade science class that year, and I knew it could kill you!

But what did mercury have to do with corn? I thought to myself. I was confused. I also had no clue what high fructose corn syrup was, so I asked my mom about it. She thought for a second and replied, "The only thing I can think of is that it's in sodas."

That was the moment where something inside of me clicked. I asked myself, *Why is there something that can hurt me really bad in my food?* I declared to my mom that I wasn't going to drink sodas anymore! I would later think of that as my light-bulb-above-the-head moment, or for those of you who like big words, my epiphany.

Soon thereafter, I decided I was going to research high fructose corn syrup to learn why stuff that can really hurt you, like mercury, was in it. I began looking for articles on the subject by simply typing those four words—"high fructose corn syrup"—into my computer's search engine. I quickly found a blog that described the process of making high fructose corn syrup. The blog said how you could not make it in your home kitchen.

I then read how you needed heavy industrial equipment like a centrifuge to make it.

As I further researched high fructose corn syrup, I started noticing other words that sparked my interest. Words like GM foods, pesticides, herbicides and chemical fertilizers. These were things I had never heard of, so I started to learn more about each one of them, too. What I would eventually come to find out was even more mind-blowing than high fructose corn syrup.

I learned about this stuff called "GM foods" or "GMOs," which are short for genetically-modified food or genetically-modified organisms. A GMO is when a DNA sequence from a plant or animal is injected into the plant of a totally different species to give it certain traits or qualities. In the instance of a tomato, for example, what happens is a gene from the Atlantic flounder (yep, a fish!) is put into a tomato's DNA. This is done so the tomatoes will grow in cold winters, which is not normal for the plant. This one example of a GMO has properly been called the "fish tomato." Sounds like something in a cheesy science fiction movie, doesn't it?!

GMOs have only been in the human diet since the mid-1990s, so we have yet to see what full effects they will have on us. Many GMO products were originally said to be safe, but then were later proven otherwise. DDT and Agent Orange also were said to be fine for human contact and later proved to cause cancer. Roundup was said to be biodegradable. Later research proved it otherwise.

Once I learned about the false advertising that companies had been pushing, I felt so deceived. I decided that I wanted to make a difference and fight these big companies.

To start, I found multiple ways to support our local farmers and organic food producers. I started looking for farmers' markets so I could meet the men and women who grow my food. I went to local food co-ops that sold the food from the farmers I got to know. I kept on researching and wanting to help, so I started volunteering at local farms. I would weed and plant and water and also feed the animals.

After a year and a half of being active in helping my family eat healthier and researching all of these things, my mom was on the computer and noticed a post that said, "Hey all you teenagers, if you have an idea worth spreading, contact us!"

My mom yelled to me, "Birke, come check this out!"

The post was by an organization called TEDx Next Generation Asheville. Mom then made a suggestion. "Why don't you send in an application since you've always been interested in the food system?"

Mom knew I really wanted to tell everyone I met how big companies were lying to us and to support our local farmers. But I looked at the form and replied, "It's only for 13 to 19 year olds. I'm only 11."

My mom smiled. "Why don't you just send in an application and see what happens?"

So I did, and a few weeks later I got an email stating that I was chosen to be one of the speakers! That was the first time I learned to not let my age be a barrier to what I wanted to achieve in life.

After months of writing my speech and trying to put such a complex subject into five minutes, I finally got it written down. This was also the first public speech I had ever done and I was very nervous. I decided I was going to memorize the speech so I could retain useful information for the audience.

Finally, the big day came. When it was my time to speak, I told the audience about my views in a speech I had titled, "What's Wrong with Our Food System and How We Can Make a Difference."

About a month later, my TEDx talk was posted online. I asked my mom to also post it on some organic companies' social media pages. After only a few hours, it had 400 views on YouTube. I was amazed that I had already reached that many people!

Then I checked again and my talk had more than 1,000 views. In only a month of being on the Internet, it hit 100,000 views!

Since that first speech, I have been fortunate to have many great opportunities and experiences to keep spreading my message. I've traveled to Italy, New York City and California, to name a few. I have also been in two documentary films and have written a children's book titled, *Birke on the Farm: A Boy's Quest for Real Food.* The most important thing to me about all of this is that I am still reaching more and more people every day with my message.

I believe that it was my passion to make a difference in the world that made that first speech possible. I hope at the end of my days long from now, even if what I feel is my ideal food system still isn't out there, that I will have made even a small difference in creating a safer and healthier world.

Birke

GET DOWN ON THE FARM!

Birke is an advocate for local/organic food and regenerative farming. Do like Birke did and visit local farms and farmers' markets, talk to the farmers and volunteer to help them—you'll be surprised at all the cool stuff you'll learn about where your food comes from. You can start by visiting BirkeOnTheFarm.com, TEDxNextGenerationAsheville.com and Ted.com.

Ryan's Well

by

Ryan Hreljac

How many steps do you take to drink clean water? Sitting in my Grade 1 class in Canada, all I had to do was take about 10 steps from my classroom to get to the drinking fountain. It was January 1998 and I was just a six-year-old kid thinking that all the kids in the world lived like I did.

My teacher, Mrs. Prest, explained that people in developing countries didn't have some of the things that we can take for granted here in Canada like a safe, comfortable home, a school to go to and clean water. She said that many people were sick and some were even dying because they didn't have access to clean water. She told us that some people walked for hours each day in Africa and sometimes it was to get dirty water! That's when we decided, as a class, to raise money to help developing countries.

We all became pen pals with another class at Angolo Primary School in Uganda, Africa. My pen pal—Jimmy Akana—wrote to me and explained how every night around midnight, he walked eight kilometers carrying a small container to collect water—dirty water—which he said looked like chocolate (but not in a good way!). The water was used for cooking and washing.

I was shocked and very upset to learn all of this. For me, getting a drink of water was easy, and I thought it should be the same for everyone. Mrs. Prest had said that $70 would build a well in Africa. So I went home and begged my mom and dad to help. After a few days, they told me I could do extra chores to earn the $70 I thought it would take to build a well and solve the world's water problems.

I worked for four months to earn my first $70. Then, I learned that it was actually going to cost $2,000 to build a well in a place like Uganda. I had a new mission ahead of me. I started speaking to service clubs, school classes and to anyone else who would listen to my story in order to raise enough money for my first well at Angolo Primary School in Uganda. And that's how my little Grade 1 project became the Ryan's Well Foundation.

It's hard to believe that now in my early twenties, my passion is still water. I recently graduated from the University of King's College in Halifax on the east coast of Canada. I studied international development and political science, and I remain involved with my foundation as a speaker and board member. I speak around the world on water issues and on the importance of making a difference no matter who you are or how old you are.

Water is essential to all life. With the support of many, Ryan's Well is committed to delivering access to safe water and sanitation. Since 1998, Ryan's Well has helped build more than 740 wells and 990 latrines (restrooms), bringing safe water and improved sanitation to more than 789,900 people.

My message to you is that I was a kid in Grade 1 and I made a difference. It doesn't matter who you are, how old you are or what you do—you can make a difference, too!

Ryan

MAKE A POSTER!

Ryan is the founder of Ryan's Well Foundation. Like Ryan, encourage your class to get involved. Organize a poster contest in your school to raise awareness about water and how to help your neighbors. Learn more about how Ryan and his team get fresh water to people around the world at RyansWell.ca.

Destiny's Peanuts

by

<u>Abigail Phillips</u>

Destiny paced around the playground keeping a steady watch of any student younger than her who came too close to the peanut patch in the school garden. When a first grader would take a small step toward the little yellow flowers, Destiny would come dashing around the greenhouse yelling, "Get away from those peanuts!"

Destiny was suspicious of anyone who expressed interest in the peanut patch, from the office secretary who asked her every day, "Those peanuts ready yet?" to the first graders running around the open field next to the garden during playtime, to neighbors living next door to the school. She was even suspicious of me, the one who taught her about growing peanuts.

I was in the midst of serving my one year as a FoodCorps service member, working with Destiny's third grade class at Pecan Park Elementary School in Mississippi. In that role, it was my job to teach the students about healthy food and where it comes from, and to help them build a sustainable school garden.

I walked into the school one rainy morning that spring with muddy boots and soggy clothes, only to be confronted by an angry Destiny. "You gave my peanuts to that man across the street! I watched you!" she exclaimed.

Startled, I explained, "No, Destiny. The peanuts won't be ready to harvest until the fall when those little yellow flowers have been pollinated and the roots have grown nobs of nitrogen, just like we talked about in class. The peanuts will take time to grow." She grumbled as she walked away. I smiled to myself.

Destiny was one of the most difficult students I worked with all year. She transferred to our school mid-semester and to prove she was tough, she constantly picked on or distracted the other students—and even me. Destiny never showed interest in the activities I presented—unless they involved a snack—and she didn't put much effort into her schoolwork. Plus, she was always upset at the last teacher who had scolded her.

As a FoodCorps service member, I was in a lucky position to not have to discipline Destiny or her classmates. Instead, I got to offer them a different type of education. Through a series of unique experiences, I inspired their curiosity in growing and eating good, wholesome food.

In March, when I brought peanuts to class for our Peanut Planting Spectacular, I began the lesson with a taste test. The students tried raw peanuts, in-shell roasted peanuts, in-shell boiled peanuts, homemade peanut butter with honey from a local farmer (talk about student satisfaction!) and a Peruvian, toasted peanut stew called *Puca Picante*. After our little peanut feast, I asked the students what part of the peanut plant they had tried. Most guessed the flower, but Destiny, obviously wanting to be different than the rest of the class, answered, "The roots."

"Destiny, you're right!" I nearly shouted. Not only had she been listening to the previous lesson on different plant parts, but by trying to stir up an argument with her classmates, she'd guessed the right answer. I proceeded to explain, "The peanuts that we eat grow off the roots, underneath the surface of the soil. They act as magnets for nitrogen, which feeds the plant or the animal that's lucky enough to find them!"

I now had their undivided attention. I asked, "So, how do y'all think we'll grow peanuts?" Answers ranged from collecting seeds from sunflowers to buying the plants at the garden store. I asked the class to collect the leftover raw peanuts and follow me out to the garden. Destiny and her classmates then watched closely as I pushed one raw peanut into the freshly turned plot. When I finished, I said to the group, "Go for it guys! Plant those peanuts, let's see what happens!" In a mob scene that made me laugh to myself, the students grabbed peanuts and pushed them into the soil.

After they had finished with their planting, I asked the group, "Who thinks we can grow peanut plants from peanuts?" Everybody, except Destiny, raised their hands. In the next few outdoor garden classes, Destiny acted aloof, but she tended to walk near the peanut patch, kicking at the dirt a bit until she noticed me watching.

Two weeks after we'd planted the peanuts, Destiny walked by the patch and squatted to poke at something. I'd been teaching the rest of the class about natural pesticides for our fruit trees and hadn't done an examination of the garden beforehand. I walked over to the peanut patch after class and sure enough, Destiny had noticed our first peanut sprouts.

During the next week of class, the students chose subjects in the garden to research, so that they could work as a class to give educated tours of the garden to the younger grades. After everyone had chosen a subject they wanted to pursue—from strawberries to worms to the greenhouse itself—I told Destiny I'd like her to focus on the peanut patch.

The students' research came together quickly for their tours. They drew pictures on the backs of cereal boxes and wrote information about their subjects next to the photos. Destiny drew a quick rendition of a peanut and said she couldn't find any information on them. Giving her the benefit of the doubt, I let it slide and simply said, "Alright."

Then, to my surprise, on the day of the garden tours, Destiny came alive!

She pulled students toward the peanut patch and practically demanded, "Look! Look down! Do you see that green leaf? That came out of a peanut! Do you believe me? You better believe me!" The students believed her; they didn't have a choice. Again, this brought a huge smile to my face.

From that day forward, Destiny kept watch over the peanut patch. Every day, she told me that she thought something had been messing with the peanuts the night before. She was the first to notice when the plants flowered and the first to ask if we could dig them up.

When the fresh crop of FoodCorps service members arrived in August, I described Destiny to the new service member at her school and asked her to make sure Destiny was included in the peanut harvest. I had transitioned into the role of fellow, which meant I was now a support staffer for the service members and was no longer serving in the schools.

The new service member at Destiny's school called one Tuesday, feeling sick and asked if I would substitute teach for her. She said, "I'd planned to do a lesson on plant parts today, but you could just harvest the peanuts with the class." I smiled.

I walked into the school and one of the first students I saw was Destiny. She exclaimed, "Ms. Phillips, that other garden lady has been taking my peanuts to the other classes!" It was good to be back.

I said, "Destiny, come with me, I'm harvesting peanuts today!"

Destiny joined the third graders I was substitute teaching and we walked toward the garden. I grabbed hold of a peanut plant, unsure myself of exactly how to harvest them, and I pulled. I shook the dirt loose from the roots and Destiny's jaw dropped.

Dangling off the root system were dozens of fully formed peanuts and, most importantly, the faith of a student newly convinced of the magnificence of her school garden.

WATCH YOUR EFFORTS GROW!

Abigail served with FoodCorps as a service member, and then as the state fellow in Mississippi for two years. Like Abigail and Destiny, you can encourage your school or neighborhood to start a garden where everyone can work together to grow cool things like peanuts and vegetables. You can even head out into your yard at home to plant your very own garden, or start smaller by nurturing a tomato plant on your porch. Then watch as your hard work and efforts grow into amazing and delicious vegetables you can eat and share! Learn more by visiting FoodCorps.org.

Abigail

Turning Green

by

<u>Sabine Teyssier</u>

It all started with food—the most basic and fundamental of items. My school cafeteria was notorious for steering away any student's appetite and was to be avoided at all costs if one craved actual sustenance. Beyond the lack of any acceptable taste, which tends to be a major component of what we choose to eat, several other important factors played into the decision a group of us took in initiating school-wide reform.

Where the cafeteria food lacked in nutritional value, it made up for it in its detrimental environmental impact. As I would soon learn, the food served to us was driven from Chicago to the San Francisco Bay Area multiple times a month, guzzling unnecessary gas and emitting tons of carbon. During my junior year, a few of my friends and I realized that a change was needed. With help from a teacher, we founded the Project Lunch Club.

Through this club, I met Judi Shils, the founder of Teens Turning Green, which is a nonprofit organization aimed at promoting sustainability by empowering youth with environmental awareness and socially just choices. As most students veered away from the foods in the cafeteria line, we decided first to tackle the problem of available snacks in the vending machine, which seemed to make up the entirety of the student body diet.

Judi attended our weekly meetings, giving us advice and helping us to implement our plans. Through much, and often futile, collaboration with our school's food service director, our club was finally able to take charge of the issue of available snacks that were both unhealthy and environmentally irresponsible. We removed the MSG-ridden brand from the vending machines and replaced it with snacks from the healthy Somersault Snack Co, which had a location in Sausalito, California—less than 20 minutes away from our school.

This was a major improvement, but I knew we had significantly more to do. I understood that in order to truly effect change among a large group of people, be it a school or an even larger community, one must first acknowledge the problem and spread awareness to those affected by it. In the case of environmental degradation, its consequences are felt on a global scale.

After identifying with Teens Turning Green's mission and admiring the great success both Judi and her daughter have had with their influential work, I was inspired to join their cause. The summer after my junior year, I interned with Teens Turning Green and became a campaign member of their most far-reaching endeavor yet, Project Green Challenge.

Project Green Challenge is a green lifestyle initiative that transforms participants from conventional to more informed and conscientious citizens of the world in 30 days. This is accomplished through challenges that focus on the importance of fair trade, gauging one's eco-footprint, conserving electricity, lessening our waste and so forth. I was able to learn about the huge impact different food products, like meat, have on systems as seemingly disconnected as our water supply. Additionally, I was exposed to the impacts of other facets of life beyond food and the ready availability of greener alternatives.

I did outreach to encourage high schools and universities across the nation and saw great feedback from almost all 50 states, as well as from several countries around the globe. My biggest role was working on the daily challenges themselves: finding fun ways to bring awareness of the impact a day-to-day lifestyle has on the environment, compiling tips and facts to guide participants through the 30-day transformation, and researching eco-leaders and eco-friendly products to give away as prizes.

With Judi, we represented Teens Turning Green at the annual Green Festival in San Francisco where we were honored for our improvements to the local community's quality of life. We also hosted a workshop at the 16th annual Peer Summit where we educated middle school students about how their choices of food and body products impacted both their health and the environment. I felt empowered by the fact that I was raising the awareness of people who could potentially become environmental advocates in the future.

During my senior year, I co-founded the Teens Turning Green club at my school to both encompass and extend beyond what our Project Lunch Club did to incorporate and "greenify" all aspects of our campus. We gave presentations to 20 classrooms about Project Green Challenge, served as campus reps and we encouraged student participation. I also spoke at a staff meeting at my former middle school where we laid the foundation for a similar club to be implemented on its campus. Our club continued to work toward improving the quality of our cafeteria food, as well as tackling the issue of cleaning products used at the school. We also helped our school in their transition to using 100-percent, post-consumer recycled paper.

The transition can be difficult when people are stuck within their habitual constraints. But as I have come to understand, when armed with the knowledge of how our actions will continue to reverberate across the earth long after we are all gone, and the positive ways in which our behavior and product selections can be transformed, people can and do strive to make good choices.

In order to continue these empowering calls to action, following high school graduation, I continued my work for Teens Turning Green, campaigning for Project Green Dorm in preparation for my own life in the dorms at New York University. I resumed my previous position outreaching for Project Green Challenge and was excited to finally practice it on my own college campus! During Earth Week 2013, I hosted the Conscious College Road Tour, which, much like how it sounds, is a college road tour designed to inform, inspire and activate students to promote sustainable practices on their campuses.

Every day, I am made aware of the potential within each one of us to effect the change we wish to see. I chose to manifest my own capacity to work toward the problem of environmental degradation. I am particularly passionate because it is a problem that does not discriminate against gender, race or religion. It affects every inhabitant of the earth. I hope to continue helping more and more people better understand how their lifestyle choices impact the planet, and how simple changes they can make will have a huge impact.

My path to environmental enlightenment, so to speak, was presented to me through a natural desire to change the healthiness, eco-friendliness and overall experience of eating in our school cafeteria. Enhancing the quality of what sustains our bodies has, in turn, taught me about sustaining our earth. I have also learned that in dealing with a problem of this magnitude, one has to take a stand locally, become confident with one's capacity and become a catalyst through which others, too, can promote change.

Sabine

HELP TURN YOUR SCHOOL GREEN!

Sabine is the co-founder of her school's Teens Turning Green chapter and Project Lunch Club. Become more eco-active at your school by learning exactly where your cafeteria food comes from, working to get healthy food options in school vending machines, asking if the cleaning products used at school are eco-friendly, and starting your own Teens Turning Green club. It's up to you to help your school be kinder to the environment. Start your journey to going green at TeensTurningGreen.org.

My Sister Alex and Her Lemonade Stand

by

Patrick Scott

I used to question how anything good could come out of something so bad.

The year was 1997. I was two years old. My younger sister, Alex, was not even a year old yet when she was diagnosed with neuroblastoma, a form of pediatric cancer.

This is my earliest memory.

When I was five, Alex held a lemonade stand to raise money for the pediatric cancer research department at her hospital. As a family, we made signs and set up the stand in our front yard. I was excited, yet I did not fully understand its importance. That first day we raised more than $2,000.

Soon after, my family moved from Connecticut to Philadelphia to be closer to the children's hospital. Every year, my sister would push to have another lemonade stand and so began our annual tradition of holding a lemonade stand to benefit childhood cancer research.

Alex, who became known as the girl who held a lemonade stand to fight cancer, began to receive attention nationwide. Other people started holding their own stands and sending the money to Alex. My family appeared on several television shows. On the *TODAY Show*, I carried a bucket around for the crowd to donate.

After we left the *TODAY Show*, my exhilaration dissipated and I returned to reality. While on air, host Matt Lauer had asked Alex if she would come back next year. Alex had answered, "Hopefully." But I could tell something wasn't right. Even though she was becoming a national hero, she was still my younger sister and seeing her this way made me feel sad and helpless. The excitement of watching our cause take off was masked by the pain of watching my sister grow sicker.

In 2004, after fighting cancer for more than seven years, my sister passed away. I was 10 years old and I was overwhelmed. I didn't think that any good could come out of my intense sadness because I was so focused on her death and not on her life. But time went on and my life kept moving.

The cause that my sister had started turned into the Alex's Lemonade Stand Foundation, which has raised more than $60 million to find a cure for other kids. Today, the foundation is still a large part of my life and I am fortunate to see firsthand the influence my sister has had on the world.

Coming to terms with the bittersweet consolation that I can feel both grief for my sister's death and joy for the extraordinary impact of her life has defined my entire outlook on life. I now have a profound appreciation that joy and sorrow can coexist, but it is up to me to let the joy define my life, not the sorrow. This lifelong journey to reconcile the worst and the best things to ever happen to me has molded me into the optimist I am today, always seeking out the positive, seeing challenges as opportunities and looking on the bright side.

In her final months, my sister said, "I'm happy for what I have, not unhappy for what I don't have."

Now, all these years later, I finally understand what she meant.

Alex

TURN LEMONS INTO LEMONADE!

Patrick is the brother of Alex Scott—founder of Alex's Lemonade Stand Foundation. Alex proved that a determined little kid and something as simple as a lemonade stand can change the world, inspire millions of people and raise lots of money to fight cancer. This is optimism at its very best. Help carry on Alex's legacy by holding a lemonade stand in your neighborhood and donating the money to your favorite charity. Learn more at AlexsLemonade.org.

CHAPTER SIX

Open Your Mind, Change the World

When we open our minds to different opinions, cultures and opportunities, we have already moved the world ahead in a positive direction.

How Soccer Will Save the World

by

Kyle Weiss

I have played soccer since I could walk. I've always loved the sport and the passion and love the world has for this beautiful game. In the beginning, I had no idea just how big of a role soccer would play in my life or that it would literally take me to the other side of the world!

In 2006, my brother Garrett and I were lucky enough to attend the International Federation of Association Football (FIFA) World Cup in Germany. One of the games we attended was Iran versus Angola. While there, the Angolan fans told us how soccer in Angola is everything. There, soccer is a way of life—it's what they enjoy the most. Here in the U.S., we often take for granted how soccer is mostly for sport and pure entertainment, not to mention big business. But in Africa, it's something completely different. For them, soccer represents hope and healing. It's a rallying point for the people to come together.

Sitting there at that game in Germany, my brother and I suddenly realized that we could help these people. Back home in Danville, California we have the best fields, the best equipment, the best everything when it comes to soccer. However, when you look at the kids in Africa, it's almost overwhelming to think about the day-to-day problems they face in their lives, such as war, life as child soldiers, diseases like HIV-AIDS and malaria, and the serious drug and alcohol problems all around them. I had no clue just how hard it was there, and how oftentimes kids are born into these unimaginable situations. What I did know is it wasn't right and I had to do something to help.

When we started out, we were just kids. I was only 13 years old at the time and Garrett was 15. We had no idea what Africa was like, or even what the people there were like. Our lives in California seemed like a million miles away from the lives of those African kids. It was a world away, for sure. We began by telling some of our friends about what we wanted to do. Originally, we decided we would take cleats and soccer balls to Africa for the kids—simple, basic things so they could play the game. Then one of our friends said, "But don't they need a field first?"

With that question, we realized how we would be able to make a real difference. It seems like a lot of movements to do good begin with a single question. That was the moment FUNDaFIELD was really born. Then and there, we decided we would build soccer fields.

The first two fields were built in a rural village in South Africa in 2008. We started there because one of our mentors, Saul Garlick, and his organization ThinkImpact, had two great schools there that really needed fields. We held our first tournament there in 2008 where all of the kids received uniforms and Coca-Cola sponsored the entire event. It was incredible—thousands of people showed up and everyone danced and had the best time of their lives. The whole community talked for years afterward about that first tournament.

Whenever we build a field in Africa, we try to put it at a school because it gives the kids a good reason to stay in school. We found that a soccer field is one of the greatest motivators for their young people. A student at one school told us, "You know, Uganda has been torn apart by war for so many years and now no one really trusts each other."

We soon realized that one of the ways people start to trust each other is by getting on that soccer field and coming together as a team. That unites a community instead of pushing it apart.

I like how our Uganda country director Ssekamwa Isaac Mugabi explains it: "The miracle of the game lies in its simplicity: it's cheap, easy to play and the rules are plain to follow. When a ball is kicked, ethnic differences, politics and hatred just melt away."

That's a pretty amazing thing to watch and be a part of. It's incredible how a field, a ball and teamwork can do so much to erase tensions and inspire progress, all toward a common goal.

Today, we have built fields throughout Africa and have more than 30 kids who are working together to raise money to build even more. From our managing directors to our directors and associates, every position at FUNDaFIELD is filled by young people who share our vision. Every FUNDaFIELD team member plans two fundraisers each year and manages their event themselves. So far, we have raised well over $200,000.

My friends and I realize we can't solve all the problems that exist in Africa and throughout the world, even though we wish we could. That's why our approach is to partner with organizations that have made it their mission to provide food, medicine, shelter and education to students. Once they have the infrastructure in place and the schools built, then we at FUNDaFIELD are able to build a safe field with equipment to play the game of soccer. Our fields offer those kids a short break each day from living with disease, hunger, poverty and other problems.

Also, soccer teaches important values and life skills like confidence, teamwork, communication, discipline, respect and fair play. These are lessons those young kids can put into play for the rest of their lives. And, for me and my fellow FUNDaFIELD team members, these are experiences that will motivate and inspire us for the rest of our lives.

Kyle

BUILD A FIELD AND THEY WILL COME!

Kyle is the co-founder of FUNDaFIELD. Like Kyle, you can use your love of sports to help build an athletic field at your school or in your neighborhood or even halfway around the world. You can also help keep an existing field clean and usable by volunteering to pick up trash, mow the lawn or work at the concession stand. Find out more about how Kyle used his passion for soccer to help people thousands of miles from his home at FUNDaFIELD.org. Also, check out ThinkImpact.com, founded by Saul Garlick when he was 18, to learn even more about having a positive impact on a global scale.

One Thing Leads to Another

by

Cortez Alexander

During a recent summer, I headed to a small town in Vermont to participate in the Iraqi Young Leaders Exchange Program as part of the School for International Training. The program brought youth from various cities in Iraq to engage in citizen diplomacy, cross-cultural communication and trans-Atlantic dialogues. Flying into nearby Hartford, Connecticut from Chicago was a big step for this young 17-year-old since it was only my second time leaving my family. Back then, I had no idea that it would be the best decision of my life.

It was 10:38 P.M. when the white cargo van carrying Iraq's youngest leaders arrived in front of my dormitory in Vermont. The anticipation of meeting the fellow teens who would be my roommates for the next 10 days was causing me to jump around, literally. I had already met my one roommate, Vishal, from London and the two of us got along great. I could not wait to now meet my two Iraqi roommates. When they finally walked in, tired after two days of traveling and adjusting to different time zones, I greeted them warmly.

Their names were Memo and Hussein. During my stay at the School for International Training, we engaged in many discussions and learned a lot about each other's cultures. What I found most fascinating was that we had many more similarities than differences. For example, apparently the music artist 50 Cent was also big in Iraq at the time. I also became aware of the many misconceptions that I myself had about Iraq and its people. From that time on, I knew that I had gained lifelong friends and a network of support from around the world.

When I returned home to Chicago with a group of Iraqi teenagers, who were going to continue their leadership training, the program technically ended for me. However, I asked the coordinator, Marian Reich, if it was possible for me to volunteer. She said yes, and so I continued this exciting new experience.

I worked with my newfound friends, commuting every day from the westside of Chicago to downtown Chicago. During that time, I unofficially became a part of the program where I was trained in leadership. I learned the art of taking action and how to write a press release. And political consultant Kevin Lampe showed us how to get people onboard to support our causes or whatever we are fighting for.

I began to feel that I should not be the only one to have this mindopening experience. Then I read about a Dream Leaders workshop sponsored by Dreams For Kids. I decided to attend the Dream Leaders event to learn even more about taking action and to again be with a diverse group of peers who were interested in changing the world.

Dream Leaders was everything I imagined—and more! I experienced a surge of energy that inspired me to develop plans to create the Arab-American Youth Leadership Conference. The goal of my conference was to bring Chicago students together with Arab-Americans from around the city.

The work to develop the conference, including locating a venue, developing the itinerary and finding a sponsoring partner, proved to be very difficult, but I completed it. However, what I failed to do was properly promote the event and, thus, no one showed up. While I felt disappointed because this was something I really wanted to have happen, that didn't necessarily mean it was a failure. I learned a lot of valuable lessons for next time.

After that experience, I figured there was something missing in my leadership arsenal, so I stepped back and took in information. I started volunteering to help other people, which brought me a sense of satisfaction unlike any other. I was able to help kids in the Dreams For

Kids programs—kids who lived on the margins of society, kids from poor families and kids with special needs.

I enjoyed volunteering, but I felt as if I should attempt to restart my ultimate vision of the Arab-American Youth Leadership Conference, using what I had learned from and since my first attempt. More Iraqis came to Chicago the following year and I started with a leadership and public speaking workshop. This time, my endeavor was a success! I felt so happy knowing that I had completed something I had originally set out to do and that I hadn't let failure stop me.

It's amazing how one thing leads to another and another and another!

The next summer, the organization WorldChicago hosted youth groups from Iraq and Mexico. This time, I had an idea to bridge the two programs and link into Dreams For Kids. That idea turned into a tennis event sponsored by the United States Tennis Association, 1WorldSports, Dreams For Kids and WorldChicago. The event brought kids from Chicago, Mexico and Iraq together to play tennis with each other at the University of Chicago in Hyde Park. It was a success, too, because everyone had fun. I can still remember looking through Facebook and seeing that one of the participants posted, "This was the best day of my life!" The post was accompanied by a big picture from the tennis event, the event that I had created.

Currently, I am an international studies major at DePaul University with an Arabic studies minor. It is funny how life works out; I never would have imagined I'd be in the places where I have been and that I would have the opportunities I have had to help so many people.

In the future, I hope to inspire and ignite a passion for leadership in others just like I have been privileged to experience. This is what I stand up for. I stand up for those who want to make a change in the world and don't know where to begin. I stand up for you, and I say no matter what you want to achieve, just start at the beginning and keep moving forward!

Cortez

USE FAILURE AS A STEPPING STONE TO SUCCESS!

Cortez is an advocate for Dreams For Kids. When his efforts in launching the Arab-American Youth Leadership Conference didn't work out the first time, Cortez didn't let that stop him. Instead, he learned from his mistakes and eventually turned his vision into a success. Never let failure stop you! Learn from it and use it as a stepping stone to the many successes waiting for you. Please visit DreamsForKids.org, SIT.edu (School for International Training) and WorldChicago.org.

Start Early and Learn for a Lifetime

by

Karen, Daniela and Stephanie Carvajalino

Our parents have been our life coaches since we were born. They have guided us from our earliest years to become entrepreneurs in business and to explore our many talents. When we were eight, seven and six years old, respectively, our parents encouraged us to start our own business. After much planning, and with $15 and a melting pot, the three of us started Chococar—a chocolate business—in our hometown located in Columbia, South America.

Chococar produced and sold chocolates in different venues like schools, private companies and local stores. Even though we earned a little money producing and selling our chocolates, making money was not the main purpose of Chococar. Our company was a teaching business where the main purpose was to learn for a lifetime. As we created Chococar, we decided that Karen was going to be the general manager, Daniela the commercial manager and Stephanie the sales executive.

There were several important things that changed our life through the process of Chococar. First, developing a sense of responsibility through real-life roles at an early age was something that marked our lives. Second, learning harmony and respect when working with family was something that will keep us together forever. Last, but not least, we left behind those things that stop many people from pursuing their dreams and goals—fears and shyness.

After one year of selling chocolates, a professor invited us to his class to share our experience. This presentation was the start of our professional lives. We realized that we had the potential to encourage, inspire and motivate students around the world to develop their talents or businesses at an early age, just as we did.

Our father, who is a master practitioner in Neuro Linguistic Programming (NLP), trained us in NLP, public speaking techniques and entrepreneurship content, which we used to put together our first official conference. One year after we launched Chococar, we hosted our first conference in Columbia called "How to Start a Business with No Money." Our first experience as speakers made us decide that this is what we wanted to do for the rest of our lives.

As we grew, studied and learned about business and NLP, we improved our conferences. We started a new part of our business, which was training people to believe in themselves and to start their financial lives at an early age. Up to this point, we had talked at more than 20 universities in Colombia, Panama and the United States. We had also spoken at numerous public and private high schools, companies, panels and congresses. Spreading our message of prosperity to young people always makes us happy and fulfills our mission.

In 2007, we understood that we needed a massive way to take our message around the world. For that reason, we wrote our first book titled, *Parents and Coaches at the Same Time*. The three of us, guided by our parents, worked together to create a book that could help parents guide their kids to success.

In a practical way, our book offers parents different tools to truly help their kids and inspire them to start their financial lives early. Our objective with our book is to create bonds and love among families. We recognize family as one of the most important things that an entrepreneur needs in order to surge. Therefore, one of the most important things that our project focuses on is improving family communication and relations.

After publishing our book, we sold it in Colombia where it was a success. Then, we decided to revise it and publish a second edition of *Parents and Coaches*, which was a success as well. Our book is in Spanish—our native language—and we are looking forward to translating it into English.

We are also now selling it online to a worldwide audience.

The three of us have learned so many lifelong lessons through the path that we have walked. Simple things like public speaking techniques and complex things like working and respecting family business relationships. We have acquired so many skills that will be useful for the rest of our lives. We are proud of what we have done, and we have enjoyed it since it all started.

We are thankful to our parents for guiding us and making us who we are today. Our deepest desire is to ensure that other families and young people around the world benefit from the business and life model that has been successful for the three of us. Having strong values, along with strong skills, will help shape the world and make it a better place for everyone.

Stephanie, Daniela and Karen

BECOME AN ENTREPRENEUR!

Karen, Daniela and Stephanie are motivational speakers and entrepreneurs. Follow the example of these three sisters and turn your skills and interests into a business, too—into something that will help, entertain or provide products or services to others. Along the way, you will learn many valuable lessons you can use throughout your life. To learn more, please visit PadresyCoaches.com.

When is Power Most Powerful?

by

Maher Alhaj

I spent the first 10 or so academic years of my life at a boarding school in Jordan, a small Muslim country in the Middle East. I had to deal with many traumatic childhood experiences growing up, such as being bullied and abused sexually, physically and in other ways. I had so much pain and anger inside of me, and I did not understand how or why this could happen.

At the same time, I had to hide my emotions, not only because I was scared and ashamed, but also because I did not want to hurt my family. I loved them very much, and I knew they had enough problems already as poor Palestinian war refugees.

I insisted I could take care of myself, and for the most part I was good at hiding my emotions. But at the end of my biweekly visitations with my family and amidst the anticipation of going back to school, I would have uncontrollable panic attacks. My heart would start pounding intensively and my throat would become so heavy that I would lose the ability to speak. I learned to avoid talking during those moments and instead, I would only gesture to say goodbye. However, once I was alone, I would emotionally collapse.

The first five years of my life at that school were miserable. I was so frustrated, and it seemed like there was no way out. I could not take it anymore and at age 11, and after some serious planning and organizing, I ran away.

I had a specific goal in mind: I fancied I would find a cave in the hills nearby, where other humans did not exist. I walked most of that first day, but my mission failed. I could not find the cave and I was very frightened and vulnerable. I spent the night at a mosque and struggled to find my way back the next day. The police officers, who were informed of my disappearance and were searching for me, scorned me and threatened that if I ever ran away again, I would go to jail.

I thought life would get better when I turned 16, the time when I would leave the boarding school. But fate had a mind of its own. I was very timid and lacked many social skills. In addition, similar to other children who go through traumatic experiences, my emotional and other psychological states were very damaged. I was also confronted with the fact that I was gay. This is a lifestyle that almost never was discussed in my surroundings in the Middle East. And when it was, it was always in very harsh tones.

To most people in that region of the world, homosexuality is a sinful choice and thus a criminal act. At that young age, I couldn't fully understand what being gay meant, nor could I change myself to be like others. No valuable theological, cultural, linguistic, scientific or other resources about homosexuality were available to me.

At first, I dedicated myself to religion, hoping to find refuge and feel better about myself. I became a very good Muslim, but my Islamic tradition did not seem to have a place for me, not as a homosexual.

Homosexuality, naturally, became the focus of my life. I knew I did not have a choice in the feelings I had about being gay, but no one around me seemed to understand that. No one around me acknowledged my existence or that of the people who were like me. Being told by others that I would go to hell for something I did not choose was devastating.

I was hopeful, however, to understand my situation and that of others, and I became determined to make it better. When I was almost 20, I moved to the United States and was admitted to the 11th grade so I could learn English and get my diploma. I also invested a lot of time navigating through the resources that I now had, which were not available to me before.

I went to a community college in 2004 and became the editor-in-chief of my college newspaper in 2005. This was a crucial turning point for me. I took that opportunity and publicly outted my homosexuality in two consecutive editorials. I wrote about my experiences as a gay Muslim in the Middle East and about my reconciliation between Islam and homosexuality.

In part, I wrote: "I refuse to perceive God as that awful harsh entity that seems to seek pleasure in torturing its creatures. I refuse to live the lies that many people see as reality. Life is good, God is good . . . To me, it is inconceivable that God forces me to do something bad then holds me responsible for doing it. No justice in that . . . If you are a homosexual, especially if you are Muslim or one who is suffering from unfair religious dogmas or harsh traditions, I wish to help you feel better about yourself . . . you are the way you are because you are meant to be that way."

By that point, I fully understood the importance of Islam in a Muslim's life and how powerful the religion is in affecting change. Therefore, in addition to my conviction that the truth of religion must transcend beyond all ignorance and hatred, I took it upon myself to find an accepting, loving and welcoming theological place for the homosexual Muslim community within the Sharia Law of Islam (the set of laws and rules that Muslims abide by, which governs all aspects of their daily lives).

To help fulfill this mission, I am publishing a book titled *Homosexuality Is Halal: The Fatwa* ("halal" means permissible within the Sharia Law of Islam, and "fatwa" means a religious ruling). The book's release was on a very special date—December 10th, the National Day for Human Rights. The book argues that homosexuality should be permissible in Islam, given the evidence from the Quran (Islam's holy book), Sunnah (Prophet Muhammad's practices and teachings) and modern science. I decided to publish the book online for free in increments at my website so it would be accessible to as many people as possible.

My book helped me take one more step forward in my journey. But I believed that providing resources that educate Muslims on Allah's loving intentions and creation for the homosexual community within Islam was not enough.

In 2011, I joined the AmeriCorps program in Chicago in a very unique partnership opportunity between two great human rights organizations—the Illinois Coalition for Immigrant and Refugee Rights (ICIRR) and Lambda Legal. This joined program was called Uniting America.

My position in this AmeriCorps program was to build bridges between native-born Illinoisans and their immigrant neighbors through volunteerism, community service and dialogue. More specifically, my focus was to build bridges between the LGBTQ community and the immigrant community here in Illinois. This AmeriCorps opportunity provided me with a lot of training. One class in particular, which was organized by ICIRR, was instrumental to what I would decide to do next. I learned how to organize the community to affect change.

With my new knowledge, I decided to dedicate my time to educate my community through organizing and advocacy about the rightful place of homosexuality within Islam. People have to act in order for them to change their predicaments—we cannot stay silent and invisible. As a result, I am currently working with an international law firm to incorporate an organization that would educate, advocate and organize Muslims and Arabs around homosexuality in Muslim and Arab societies.

Before I end, I would like to share a favorite quote from *Invisible Man* by American author Ralph Ellison. It has been a source of inspiration to me. He writes, "All my life I had been looking for something and everywhere I turned, someone tried to tell me what it was. I accepted their answers too, though they were often in contradiction and even self-contradictory. I was naive. I was looking for myself and asking everyone except myself questions which I, and only I, could answer."

No matter where you come from or what challenges you are facing, find your own calling and unleash your powers. My journey has taught me that true power is most powerful when it comes from within.

Maher

NEVER BE INVISIBLE!

Maher is an activist, writer, artist and former Ameri-Corps fellow. Take a page from Maher's book and never let anyone intimidate you or prevent you from standing up for what you believe in. Write, speak and act on your beliefs! Please visit homosexualityishalal.com, Ameri-Corps.gov, ICIRR.org (Illinois Coalition for Immigrant and Refugee Rights) and lambdalegal.org.

Where Does Meat Come From?

by

Mariama Taifa-Seitu

The question "Where does meat come from?" struck me as disturb-
ing at 14 years old. It was an uneasy and perplexing concept because it was
something I had never questioned, and never thought to question. Now
a student at Sarah Lawrence College in New York, studying agricultural
development, I am proud of my curiosity back then to delve into that question of where meat really came from. As a young adult, I chose to stand
up for what I believed in, and what I knew to be the right direction from
which agriculture should be approached.

Throughout my high school years at School Without Walls Senior
High School in Washington, D.C., I worked on spreading awareness about
the issue of factory farms. Factory farms, although overlooked by much of
the global population, take a detrimental toll on society and contribute to
environmental degradation, violations to animal welfare and serious human health problems.

Simply put, factory farms are meat production industries made
for profit and corporate gain, and it is in their interest that the public
stay at a comfortable distance, far removed from the realities of the
business of meat. I strongly believe that all beings have inalienable
rights of freedom and life, and I have chosen, like many others, to be a

vegetarian because of ethical and health issues.

I was thankfully raised in a health-conscious environment and grew up without ever tasting red meat. During my freshman year of high school, I read an article on the modern meat industry and became aware of the reality of meat production in this country and around the world. I started looking at the political side of agriculture today—how policies in the globalized distribution of food were doing more harm to society than good.

I stopped eating turkey and seafood and turned vegetarian. I was extremely proud to practice compassionate and ethical eating for the planet, my health and farm animals. But it wasn't enough. I wanted everyone to be aware of the fact that our agricultural system was facing a crisis and that, as a nation, we can stop corrupting our health and the environment by not supporting agribusinesses. I knew I couldn't change the way America handles animal agriculture, but I could at least make a change in my own community.

At my high school, every senior is required to create a senior project for which they pick a controversial topic to argue. For my project, I researched the impact of the consumption of factory farm meat products on the environment and human health. In my project, I argued that the rise of meat-causing diseases, environmental degradation and meat contamination were directly linked to factory farming. My presentation was controversial from the start, and I was faced with disdain and grossed out faces from my fellow students. I learned that people would rather be far removed from their problems than face the truth.

For my senior project, I had to set up a concrete product—a visual presentation of my paper. I had a lot of different ideas about what I wanted to do for my product, from investigating a local factory farm in Virginia (not the safest idea) to rallying my classmates to try vegetarianism for a month. After much research, I decided to administer a "feed-in." I would distribute free vegetarian food and literature in front of eating establishments that lacked vegetarian friendly options or that profited from animal abuse. I believed I would make the message of my senior project clear and concise by organizing a feed-in to promote food safety and sustainable agriculture.

I worked to make my project the very best I could. To help me prepare for my own feed-in, I volunteered with the nonprofit organization Compassion Over Killing for their feed-in in front of Subway, encouraging the restaurant to include a delicious Tofurky sandwich on the menu. I got a good feel from working with Compassion Over Killing for how I should administer my own feed-in.

I researched fast food restaurants that were known for animal abuses, and I came across one of the biggest offenders. I learned that this particular fast food restaurant uses factory farms and is one of the few that refused to adopt an animal welfare program.

After learning about these discrepancies, I became inspired to stand up for my community. On December 4, 2012, I stood outside of this fast food restaurant in my community and handed out to passersby free fried tofu I had cooked, as well as vegetarian starter kits. My goal was to inform others of the inhumane abuses the fast food restaurant imposes on factory farm animals and to promote healthy eating. Thanks to the Compassion Over Killing feed-in, I understood exactly what to do, what to say and what to have at my own feed-in.

Hoping to get my message in front of the media and make it a success, I contacted a reporter from the local *AFRO-American Newspaper* to see if she could write an article about my senior project. My efforts landed a spot as a feature article in the Washington, D.C. edition of the paper. Much to my surprise, the fast food restaurant even commented on the article. The article ran for several weeks in the paper as one of the most viewed articles and the controversy over my topic sparked comments from all over the world!

I never thought I could evoke a debate about food justice simply from my inspiration and interest in sustainable food policies. I more fully realized the impact of my work against inhumane and inefficient agricultural practices when I was later invited to be the featured speaker at the SEED Festival in Baltimore. I spoke about my senior project and the benefits of sustainable and organic agriculture. The executive director of Compassion Over Killing, Erica Meier, then contacted me and invited me to be a featured speaker at the annual DC VegFest in Washington, D.C.!

To stand up and make a change in my community was the greatest experience I could have ever imagined. Activism by young people is advocacy for change at its best, and I am appreciative of all of the support I received when I dedicated myself to the issue of today's agriculture. Community and youth empowerment are intrinsically linked, and I believe that educating the public is the first step to activism. As a young activist, I had to be self-reflective and conscious of my own individual actions. I had to check myself and make sure I was not violating my own ethics, a difficult feat in a society such as ours.

I believe that consumers who are educated about factory farms can make healthier and more humane choices for themselves, rather than allowing agribusinesses to continue to mislead the American public. Killing animals is an act of violence and exploitation, and just as society's moral development has evolved, it is time to recognize that the consumption of factory farm animals is wrong.

Mariama

ASK QUESTIONS AND SEEK THE ANSWERS!

Mariama is an animal and agriculture activist. She started her mission with a simple, yet very important, question. What questions do you have about the world around you? Ask them—you may be surprised where the answers will lead you! To help animals and learn more about the food you eat, please visit COK.net (Compassion Over Killing), DCVegFest.com and TheSeedFestival.com.

Jumping Over Obstacles

by

Natasha A. Abdin

High school allowed me the opportunity to thrive and be myself, but most importantly, it helped me to see how unfair a lot of things in life can be. Largely, society faces the same issues teenagers face in high school. I had to fight for my concerns to be heard and to be recognized for what I saw as unjust.

While high school presents various opportunities to thrive, there are still many personal obstacles that one has to overcome. I was determined that my goals would be achieved, and this became easier to do the more I realized my own personal power and uniqueness among the crowd. I tried to understand how my power could positively influence others and how I could move forward on good acts of faith. I saw that with some extra hard work and continued commitment to the projects that inspired me, I could make a difference in my school and community.

My freshman year consisted of keeping to myself and not really communicating with those who intimidated me. This meant spending my lunch periods eating at a deserted lunch table or hiding out around the girl's bathroom. High school life as a freshman was lonely to say the least, but then came my sophomore year and I learned how to better navigate my high school environment. I was no longer one of the new kids, and was, therefore, able to stand a little steadier on my own two feet.

I joined student clubs like Drama, Ecology and the Human Relations Council where I met like-minded individuals. The best part of my second year in high school was that I was no longer eating lunch by myself, and that I could volunteer at places like the Yearbook Club to pass the time. In fact, most of my spare time was spent in the library assisting the librarian or working in the student counselor's office, which I guess you could say gave me a sense of purpose in my desire to help other lost students like me.

By my junior year, I had become relatively well known—dare I say even popular—among my circle of friends. I formed the habit of writing an informative letter to my principal each semester as to the problems I witnessed. I included possible solutions to improve these issues, which included the excessive time it took students to wait in various lunch lines without knowing what type of mystery meat was being served on the lunch menu (especially as our diverse population of students included Muslims, who do not consume pork). I also encouraged students to get involved in school life, to sign petitions or volunteer their time.

One of the most rewarding projects that I organized was playing host to bestselling author Alex Sanchez for an educational workshop. As it would turn out, the big problem with this was that the author happened to be gay. This small factor was met with much more criticism by the administration than I had ever anticipated. Teachers bluntly told me that the school would never allow such an event to take place, stating that the school's budget was frozen and they would not be spending money on a "gay author." More to the point, I was told that parents would be overtly outraged if a public school allowed such a thing to happen. It was as if I were asking a sex offender to visit my high school.

My first step in planning this educational event was to draft a formal proposal, which included the purpose of the author's visit, a school library copy of one of his recently published novels and a list of his awards and achievements. Next, I met with the administrative staff where their concerns were addressed and guidelines were implemented regarding the upcoming event. One condition of the visit was that all of the students attending the workshop would need to turn in a signed parental consent form, which insured that parents knew that the author was "a homosexual." I felt that not only was this form insulting to the author's credibility, but it was also demeaning to him as a human being.

I strongly opposed this provision, stating that it would severely limit the attendance at this very important event. To add to my frustration, another condition was put into place stipulating that a minimum of 30 students would have to commit to this event before the school would agree to host it. Even with all of these obstacles, I pulled off the event and it was an overwhelming success! I was so happy and proud of what I had accomplished, even when others told me that it would never work out.

Finally, my senior year came around, and I had reached the mountaintop, but there was still a lot of work to be done. While volunteering at my school, several students had approached me about their concerns regarding feeling unsafe and bullied on campus. Teachers failed to address derogatory comments exchanged in their classrooms, which allowed bullies to continue getting away with their taunting behaviors. These students wanted a safe place where they could talk openly about how they felt for not being straight or for being perceived as gay.

I looked into what we could do to make our school more accepting of everyone and learned about the Gay-Straight Alliance (GSA). GSA student clubs exist all over the United States, found mainly on school campuses. If we had a GSA at our school, I knew it would allow students to openly discuss their insecurities, personal troubles and, chiefly, human rights issues promoting the understanding and tolerance of people's sexual orientation. I found two open-minded teachers who were receptive to this idea, pushed for an early administrative hearing and presented this concept to the student union for their approval. A few months later, a GSA club was formed at our school and it was humbling to see how this club helped so many of my peers.

What started out as a horrible first year of high school ended up becoming a four-year experience that taught me lifelong lessons of kindness, generosity and friendship. Now, as a graduate student and the proud founder of my own nonprofit organization—called The Abdin's Center for Empowerment—I realize that if I had the chance to go back to high school, I probably would not change any of my struggles or successes. Those experiences, good and bad, helped to mold me into the strong person I am today and will continue to be.

Natasha

OBSTACLES JUST MEAN YOU HAVE
TO JUMP A LITTLE HIGHER!

Natasha is the founder of The Abdin's Center for Empowerment. Natasha didn't let the obstacles she faced in school stop her from achieving her goals, and neither should you. When faced with an obstacle or challenge, figure out how best to navigate your way over, around or straight through it! Please visit TheAbdinsCenter.org, AlexSanchez.com and GayStraightAlliance.org.

CHAPTER SEVEN

Power to the People

Inside each one of us is the ability to change the world by empowering people from every walk of life to lead happier, healthier and more awesome lives.

The Million Girl Revolution

by

<u>Dallas Jessup</u>

W hen I was a freshman in high school, I founded the organization called Just Yell Fire. It all started when news reports of high-profile kidnappings and murders of girls led me to make a film titled *Just Yell Fire* to teach girls about the unique dangers we face and how to stay safe in a sometimes difficult world.

I named the film and my nonprofit Just Yell Fire because when you're in trouble and you yell "Help!," people tend to think you're playing—too many kids who are horsing around yell "Help!" and bystanders ignore them, kind of like car alarms. Likewise, if you yell, "I'm being taken!," people don't want to get involved. They too often think of this as a domestic issue and don't want to get in the middle of it. But if you yell, "FIRE!," you'll grab their attention. Bystanders' personal safety instincts or curiosity kick in. They look to see where the fire is.

What your attacker doesn't want are witnesses or attention. So yelling "FIRE!" brings the most attention to your situation and sometimes that alone will scare the attacker off. Also, and maybe more importantly, when a person is attacked, everything happens so fast that the natural instinct is to freeze up. You forget everything. But if you can remember to yell "FIRE!," that can act as a trigger and all the techniques you have learned will come back to you so you can get yourself out of the situation.

Using "FIRE!" as a trigger is an effective tool in saving your life. And that's why I chose Just Yell Fire for our cause—to help everyone be safer in the world around them.

When the word spread of what we were doing with the film, a professional crew and 100 extras volunteered to help. Even actors Josh Holloway and Evangeline Lilly from the television show *Lost* lent their talents to the project. The film went viral and because of its worldwide success, we created the nonprofit Just Yell Fire to both raise awareness and to organize our efforts to spread the stay-safe information to schools, colleges, crisis shelters, police agencies and elsewhere. The media picked up on this and we quickly grew across 65 countries.

The idea for the sequel, called *Just Yell Fire: Campus Life*, came about when I left for college at age 17. I soon learned that girls heading off to college, typically living away from home for the first time like I was, are prepared for the academics, but pretty much are clueless when it comes to the social and real-world side of the experience. They expect their idolized *Gossip Girl* environment with no hiccups or danger, but the reality is that one in three will experience dating abuse and one in four will be a victim of physical violence. Few know they have rights, and even fewer know how to stand up for those rights.

When more than 1.6 million girls downloaded the first *Just Yell Fire* film and many later reported getting away from violent or abusive situations because of what they learned, we knew that an online film made by girls for girls could have a big social impact. Also, I have found from speaking at schools and colleges around the country that girls listen to someone their own age while they ignore warnings from parents or teachers.

Thus, the reason for the sequel, which was one of the most exciting things I've ever done. As a scriptwriter, I had to create a realistic narrative that would convey our stay-safe messages in a way that would hold the attention of college-age girls. And I had to keep the film's length under an hour. The pressure was on because of the importance of the message and knowing that if it was good enough, we could once again connect with and protect millions of girls around the world.

It took a full year of writing (and rewriting) after my college classes, late at night and when I was on the road for speaking engagements. We then had to gather the resources to turn the script into the *Just Yell Fire: Campus Life* film. Maybe the hardest part was making it all happen with almost no money as we're a nonprofit with very limited funding. But we were really lucky to find some experienced actors who readily volunteered, thanks to the assistance from a casting agent who donated her time. The director from the first film stepped up again, as well as the film company.

Then we had to deal with the seemingly endless details like arranging locations, wardrobe, equipment, transportation, legal releases, food for the crew and everything else, but somehow it all came together. The word got out and more than a dozen entertainment and sports celebrities also jumped in to do cameos in the film.

Countless hours later, we put *Just Yell Fire: Campus Life* online as a free download and also started rolling it out to universities across the country and around the world. My sorority, AOII, partnered with us as well so that their 160 chapters could offer the program to their schools and their sisters.

Just Yell Fire is now known as the "Million Girl Revolution." This all happened with an amazing team and great communication and technology combined with the power of a simple idea. The simple idea is that neither parents nor police can be everywhere, so girls are on their own in an often-dangerous world. We have discovered that if we empower girls to know their rights and give them a hour's worth of street fighting training, any girl of any size can get the few seconds she needs to get away from an attacker—regardless of the attacker's size or strength. I have a black belt in Tae Kwon Do and am a 2nd degree instructor in Filipino Street Fighting.

We've learned that girls think they need a black belt and years of training to be effective at self-defense. They are universally shocked that they can learn enough in one hour to get out of almost any situation with just a few street-fighting tools. An attacker of any size can be disabled for a few seconds with an eye gouge, a groin slap or a strategic bite. These techniques give girls the chance to get away and run, and that's our advice: don't stay and fight. Get yourself out of danger and escape as fast as you can.

My biggest challenge is probably the sheer number of predators out there. There are 568,000 registered sex offenders in the U.S. alone. It seems like they are everywhere. That's the point I really try to drive home—I don't want girls to be afraid to live their lives. They need to be aware and prepared.

During the more than 200,000 miles I have traveled so far on behalf of my nonprofit, I am frequently asked to give my best advice for someone interested in getting involved with a cause. It's simple: Do what you love to do.

This is a lot of work, but it is very much worth it. You can't do your best if you don't like what you are doing. Find what makes you angry and change it. It doesn't have to be big or international. It can be something local, it can be some injustice right in your hometown or school. I wrote the book, *Young Revolutionaries Who Rock,* to spotlight some incredible kids who took on impossible social crises and made a big difference. The message of the book, and so much of what I do with my organization, is that one kid can (and should) make a difference.

Get involved now. This is the best time to become active in social issues. We are young and we don't have the responsibilities that adults have. We have the energy and the time. All it takes is effort. If we all get involved, we can change the world!

The famous cultural anthropologist Margaret Mead said, "Never doubt that a small group of thoughtful, committed citizens can change the world. Indeed, it's the only thing that ever has."

Dallas

START YOUR OWN REVOLUTION!

Dallas is the founder of Just Yell Fire, also known as the Million Girl Revolution. Like Dallas says, your time is now— get involved with a cause that speaks to you and inspires you to make positive changes in your school, your community and the world. By doing so, you, too, can start a revolution! Join Dallas' revolution at JustYellFire.com.

We Are Today's Leaders

by

Daniel Kent

This is a story about 3,500 teens who have shown that while any one person can make a difference, together we can change the world!

While in middle school, I was teaching computer and Internet skills at our public library. One day, a senior citizen approached me and said it was so sad how his wheelchair-bound neighbors could not leave their independent-living facility to learn how to use the Internet and email their grandchildren. That sparked an idea, and I promised to help.

After doing some research, I found that digital inclusion, which means digital access for all, regardless of age, was a national problem and no organization was out there to help change that. So I decided that I would. I took the $4,000 that I had been saving to buy a car and instead formed a corporation. Together with my friends, we founded Net Literacy, a student-managed digital literacy nonprofit where teens comprise 50 percent of the board of directors and perform all of the volunteering.

Many of the senior citizens whom we have taught are mobility impaired, lack reliable transportation or have tried taking computer classes and were left feeling as if they had failed. Consequently, our organization decided to construct public computer labs inside the seniors' own independent living facilities to encourage participation and to make computers part of their home. We developed training guides that were easy to follow, written in a large font, contained many illustrations and excluded needless technical jargon. Most importantly, we changed the teaching model by working with each resident on a student-to-senior citizen basis for two to three months. Friendships were established as the seniors "adopted" the friendly student volunteers. And as seniors crossed through the digital divide, the student volunteers passed through the intergenerational divide.

My most memorable experience occurred after months of teaching a resident who had memory problems and who seemed cold to me at times. Suddenly, she became teary-eyed during a lesson. Then she told me how she had been so scared that she was too old to learn to use computers, but now realized she was wrong.

Kind families began to donate dozens of used computers to us so we could refurbish them and use them to build computer labs. However, we were at a loss to find a way to obtain the hundreds and even thousands of computers we needed to really be able to make a difference. That's when I decided to take a chance. I called the mayor of our city, explained what we were doing and asked him if we could conduct a computer drive inside City Hall. He hesitated a few seconds then said, "Yes." Next, I called local newspapers, asking them to publicize the event. They generously printed stories announcing our computer drive and detailing our student-empowered nonprofit. We were thrilled when our first computer drive netted 150 computers!

The next week, a caravan of our parents' cars and vans began moving the computers and monitors from City Hall to my home. My basement and garage became our computer-refurbishing facility and my friends and I worked after school repairing and relicensing the computers.

Our supply of computers continued to grow as we conducted more computer drives around the city and in town halls throughout our county. Four of the communities issued official proclamations supporting our work, and our nonprofit of middle school student volunteers became front-page news in *The Indianapolis Star*.

During high school, Net Literacy continued to add new programs, and thousands of students at dozens of schools became volunteers. For example, we added an Internet safety program where teens use straight talk to discuss real issues with younger students and their parents in the schools. We prioritized the safety issues and produced videos to engage teens and encourage good decision making.

We were on a roll. The state superintendent of public instruction agreed to join our honorary board and held a press conference in the state-house to jointly announce our new $100,000 per year public service announcement initiative. The Indiana General Assembly passed a resolution encouraging public access channels to carry our online safety programming. National online safety websites asked us to become bloggers, and I was invited to speak about Internet safety in conferences ranging from Mountain View, California to Moscow, Russia.

Net Literacy is an innovative problem solver. After visits to Hong Kong and Denmark, I learned that funding limitations had shuttered digital inclusion associations and diminished the international sharing of digital inclusion best practices between governments and nonprofits. I believed that a website that promoted international digital inclusion would be effective, so I developed DigitalLiteracy.org, an international best practices website.

To date, we now have relationships with Internet associations representing 270,000 Internet companies on six continents. And Net Literacy was awarded the 21st Century Achievement Award by *Computerworld* as "the most innovative application of IT to extend the distribution of digital information and access to web-based programs and services."

The Net Literacy model also rewards our own student volunteers by teaching STEM skills (Science, Technology, Engineering and Math), leadership and life and job skills as they serve their communities. Several colleges now recognize every Net Literacy volunteer by providing them $5,000 in scholarships.

Today, Net Literacy provides $1.2 million in services annually. There are 3,500 student volunteers who have increased computer access to more than 225,000 individuals. The organization has also donated 24,000 computers, to date. Two American presidents have honored our accomplishments and the FCC cited three of our programs in the National Broadband Plan presented to Congress. The European Union's Study on Digital Inclusion also cited Net Literacy as one of the "91 most promising digital models in the world." Our honorary board includes the governor and a bipartisan group of seven current and former members of Congress who all believe in youth social entrepreneurship, student success and the importance of increasing digital inclusion and digital literacy. Half of our working board is comprised of students, with the other half comprised of educators and leaders from socially-minded corporations like Intel, Google, Microsoft and Cisco Systems.

Much work remains because those who are offline are being left behind. Tomorrow, those without access to broadband will be, in a sense, disabled and unable to access the increasing number of services that are migrating to the web and are not available to those left offline. Those who are disconnected will become poorer, detached from rich information and less able to compete in school, in the workforce and in life.

When I founded Net Literacy, I thought that it was an act of giving back to others. But I have learned more than anyone as these experiences have crystallized my priorities and aspirations.

Net Literacy is the story of 3,500 student volunteers who have proven that we are not tomorrow's leaders—we are today's leaders.

Daniel

BE A LEADER AND CROSS THE DIVIDE!

Daniel is the founder of Net Literacy. In middle school, Daniel saw a need among senior citizens for better computer skills and literacy, and so he crossed the generational divide while helping his elders cross the digital divide. Find a divide that exists around you—at home, at school or in your community—and then lead the way to the other side. Find out more about Daniel's journey at NetLiteracy.org.

The Luck of the Draw

by

Isabella Gelfand

The din of applause was almost drowned out by the pounding of my heart. As I stepped up to the podium with sweaty palms, the applause died out, signaling that the audience was ready for me to speak. I had just been introduced as the youngest feminist in the banquet hall. I was 14. As I stood, knees shaking, at the Feminist Majority Foundation's "Women, Money, Power" Forum being streamed on C-SPAN from Washington D.C., I couldn't keep from asking myself, *How did I get here?*

I remembered when my mother handed me the list of clubs offered at my new middle school. I was almost 12 years old and would be entering the sixth grade.

I skimmed the list until something caught my attention: Girls Learn International (GLI), an organization that works to end poverty through girls' education. I learned that the chapter at my school would be communicating with girls at a partner school in Afghanistan. That sparked my interest. The opportunity to discover a world outside my town was exciting!

By exchanging projects with girls at our partner school—Abdullah Bin Omar School, located in an area where the Taliban had denied girls access to an education in Afghanistan—I learned how much these girls value their education. For example, in one letter our school received, an Afghanistan student wrote, "My goal is to be a useful individual for my people. It takes a long time to come to school, but it is a road I love to take."

GLI chapters focus on human rights and human rights violations worldwide. Because of gender inequality, millions of girls are being denied access to education and are vulnerable to gender-based violence. I learned that the best investment for the future of our world is to unlock the potential of girls whose voices have been silenced and whose rights have been stolen. When a girl is educated, she is empowered to make her own decisions and stop the cycle of poverty.

At a workshop at my school, I learned the Taliban has a list of laws that deprive girls of everyday freedoms. When a girl breaks just one of these laws, she is punished with public beatings, shootings, stoning or amputation of limbs. During one workshop activity, each club member began with 10 Hershey's Kisses, representing basic freedoms like laughing, showing your face in public, and attending school, work or even a doctor's appointment. We then had to throw away one Kiss for each Taliban law we had broken that day. When we lost a Kiss, it symbolized that not only were our rights stolen, but that under the Taliban, we also might have been killed. We weren't even halfway through the list of laws when everyone's Hershey's Kisses were gone. The thought of living bound in chains of oppression like that was unimaginable to me. I am happy to share that while I was in middle school, we raised $1,000 for our partner school at the end of each year so the students there would have a chance for a brighter future.

In eighth grade, I was elected president of my GLI chapter, was a member of the New York Area Junior Board and was selected as one of GLI's student delegates to participate in the Commission on the Status of Women (CSW) at the United Nations. The CSW is where women's issues are discussed among world leaders and policies related to women and girls are created. I had the opportunity to work with a group of girls from around the world to draft the 2012 Girls' Statement, highlighting heartbreaking difficulties rural girls face daily.

The CSW was the most incredible experience of my life. I've always lived in an upper-middle class, mostly-white suburban town, sheltered from the horrific violations against girls around the world. All of a sudden, the issues I studied in GLI were real and personal. They were embodied by the incredibly courageous girls I met, like Thando from the Zulu tribe in South Africa, who told me that in her village, polygamy—which is a husband who has more than one wife—was common and how damaging the practice was to women. Thando's grandfather was told by others that educating his granddaughter was a waste of money.

These issues impact girls like Agatha from Uganda, who described how, in her community, abortion is punishable by death. These issues impact thousands of young girls who are bought and sold as sex slaves, even here in the United States. I learned from a panelist how human trafficking brainwashes its victims by beating, drugging and threatening them into cooperation. When they can no longer be sold, they are disposed of. Hearing this, I could barely speak—it broke my heart. It outraged me that even in my own country, girls' childhoods and futures are being stolen, leaving them with scars that brand their souls forever.

These experiences made me realize how lucky I was to be born into a family that loved me and kept me safe. But that was just the luck of the draw. By the same luck, I could have been born elsewhere, ending up in a child marriage or sold as a sex slave. The girls born in communities where they are not valued and fall victim to abuse are trapped by circumstances, not by any fault of their own.

At the CSW, I was moved by the fact that the women affected by these issues are not viewing themselves as victims—they are survivors who are speaking up, standing up and fighting for a better tomorrow. I wanted others to hear the heartbreaking, yet inspiring stories of the courageous people I'd met. So I wrote a one-woman play, *Trumpet Calls*, focusing on girls' rights around the world and my personal experience with GLI.

Each character in my play is a woman whom I have either interviewed or whose speeches moved me to action. I performed a portion of *Trumpet Calls* at my school, and drew tears and a standing ovation from the audience. That night I was on top of the world, not because I performed well, but because the issues that affect so many innocent girls were being realized by the people in that room. I knew that the audience wasn't really applauding me—they were applauding the cause. That is when I understood the power of awareness.

So as I stepped up to the podium at the "Women, Money, Power" Forum, I could feel the presence of each girl who touched my heart and moved me to action. As I began to share the story of my sisters at Abdullah Bin Omar School in Afghanistan, I reflected on how I had gotten there and I realized that this is where I wanted to be, standing up and speaking out until no more children are deprived an education.

Girls' education cannot be put on the back burner anymore. It's time for us to choose a better tomorrow. In order for women to gain the freedoms they deserve, it is critical for all to be on board. The equalization of the sexes cannot be labeled as a women's issue. It requires the involvement of every nation and every individual.

Isabella

BECOME AWARE!

Isabella is an active member of the Girls Learn International chapter at her school. Like her, become aware of the issues and challenges facing others at your school, in your community and around the world. Then figure out the best way to help those in need. Become more aware of the world around you by visiting GirlsLearn.org.

Empower Orphans

by

Neha Gupta

Imagine a life of having to face the world alone, without a mother or father. What if you did not have adequate money to support yourself, leaving you to beg or steal food and search for shelters? Unimaginable, isn't it?

We go through our lives in search of the finest things, while we blatantly overlook the stigmas faced by those less fortunate. How then is our world supposed to balance? There is no way, unless we notice this problem and take action. This realization struck me early in life. Not only did I feel empathetic, but I took a stand, forming a nonprofit organization called Empower Orphans, where we strive to improve the lives of orphaned and underprivileged children globally.

Today, at age 17, my life has transformed into a world centered on helping thousands of children. This has taught me valuable lessons about myself, human nature and the need for change.

To date, my organization has donated more than $1 million and positively impacted the lives of more than 25,000 orphaned and disadvantaged children:

★ In the area of education, we have sponsored the education of 100 children, established five libraries with 15,500 books, set up four computer labs, started a science center and created a sewing center in India with 60 sewing machines at an underprivileged school. This center enables young women and girls to learn a skill, facilitating their ability to earn a living and stand on their own two feet.

★ In the area of healthcare, Empower Orphans convened an eye and dental clinic, which benefited more than 360 underprivileged children in India, sponsored polio surgeries for children, donated 100 vanloads of home goods to underprivileged children and their families in Pennsylvania and provided diapers to more than 5,000 children in Bucks County, Pennsylvania. We also installed a water well and a water purification system to provide clean drinking water and donated toys, food, clothes, books, shoes and bicycles to thousands of children.

★ In the future, I intend to widen my circle of influence. In India, I plan on establishing additional libraries and computer labs at underprivileged schools, and to double the number of children whose educations we sponsor. Efforts to help critically at-risk girls earn a living will also continue through the expansion of the sewing center and by increasing the number of machines that are donated to participants.

★ In the United States, I will continue to provide vanloads of home furnishings to underprivileged families in my local community and start additional libraries and computer labs in the Philadelphia area. A number of corporate sponsors have already signed up to assist in these efforts.

One of my fondest memories was being able to personally view the difference I made in someone's life. When I went to India a couple of summers ago, one of the girls, whom we had given a sewing machine to through the sewing center, invited me to her home. Her house was a single room shared among five people. She informed me with great pride and gratitude that her earnings as a seamstress allowed the family to attain electricity for their house for the very first time. This basic amenity allowed her to work at night. It also enabled her brother to study for and pass an electrician's qualifying exam. Both of their efforts added to the family's finances. Knowing that I had been able to make a vast difference in someone's life gave me tremendous satisfaction.

Through my experiences with Empower Orphans, I have not only learned several useful lessons and skills, but I've become all the more aware of the need for humans to step up and change the world. Each and every person in this world has the power to change society, and we all need to put this power to use to fight against the problems faced by our world.

Neha (back row)

EMPOWER YOURSELF AND OTHERS!
Neha is the founder of Empower Orphans. Follow Neha's example—empower yourself with knowledge by learning about the plights and needs of others, and then empower those individuals by lending a helping hand and encouraging them to pursue their dreams. Start your road to empowerment at EmpowerOrphans.org.

Blossom Power!

by

Abi Whitmore, Alicia Nikifarava, Aspen Bellefeuille, Joanie Ellis, Jordan Pittman and Marissa Shevins, with Roweena Naidoo

It was a bright August morning in Denver. Outside was a hub of activity—birds chirping, bicycles whizzing by, children laughing. Inside our classroom, however, the mood was less than cheerful. We were being led through a session on the history of feminism in the United States.

In our little classroom, we were enraged. We are a small group of students, all young women from different schools, from various parts of Colorado, with a diversity of experiences. Yet, as upset as we were, we were glad that a program like The Blossom Project existed to reveal these issues to us. The Blossom Project is the flagship program of Fempowered. It is a learning, leadership, advocacy and philanthropy program for high school girls.

The history of feminism should have been a lesson wrought with inspiration and motivation for us, celebrating the journey of overcoming obstacles. Instead, we seemed fixated on the obstacles. Perhaps it was because the struggles of women over 100 years ago seemed to still exist today.

On July 4, 1776, the United States declared independence from Great Britain. It was to become the touchstone of democracy—a country that embraced the ideals of life, liberty and the pursuit of happiness. Sadly, women didn't receive the right to vote until 144 years after that independence. And because of discriminatory voting practices, African-American women received the right to vote just a few decades ago.

We heard about many excuses for not enfranchising women. Among our favorites are the long-held beliefs that voting would lead women to become more masculine or promiscuous; that women were far too delicate to comprehend the voting decisions and would go mad; and that women didn't need to vote, because they would vote like their husbands anyway. Women were not taken seriously. It is no wonder that up until 1918, the constitution of the state of Texas read that voting was open to anyone, except idiots, imbeciles, aliens, the insane and women.

The dawn of the women's movement was exciting. But some husbands were threatened and used violence as a means of chastising or controlling their wives. This was legal and even expected. Women had no remedy against it. In fact, organizations to prevent animal cruelty and cruelty toward children were established long before any organization that helped women who were being abused. That seemed to us to be an unfortunate trend in our society's history.

In 1979, President Jimmy Carter formed the Office of Domestic Violence, but in 1981 President Reagan dismantled it. In 1994, Congress passed the Violence Against Women Act (VAWA). For the first time, this groundbreaking legislation afforded women the federal right to sue for gender-based violence. However, in 2012, VAWA's renewal was opposed by conservative Republicans who objected to extending the Act's protections to same-sex couples and opposed provisions allowing abused illegal immigrants to claim temporary visas. In April 2012, the Senate voted to reauthorize the VAWA. The House passed its own measure, leaving out provisions of the Senate bill that would protect gay men, lesbians, American Indians and illegal immigrants who were victims of domestic violence. Reauthorization remains in question as of this writing.

During our yearlong program, we, known simply as "The Blossoms," learned about issues that became important to us and are being faced in our community. The focus of our group is on reproductive justice, human trafficking, homelessness, teen dating violence, the media's representation of girls and the cliff effect, where a small increase in income leads to a disproportionate drop in public aid. We also work with Colorado experts to create advocacy projects, so that we can affect positive change in our communities.

Through the philanthropy component of our program, we raise funds that are distributed to organizations working on the issues we identified. The Blossoms created a funding application and invited organizations to apply. When considering these funding applications, we conduct site visits before making funding decisions. Next year, we will look at the same issues from a national perspective, and the following year we will take a global view.

The Blossom Project has certainly opened our eyes to so many things. And yet we have to wonder why these topics are not shared in our schools. But then it dawned on us: history is often written by the Victors . . . not the Victorias!

How then are we to know about women like Sybil Luddington? In 1777—at age 16—she rode her horse through New York and Connecticut warning that the British were coming. Even though she did the same thing as Paul Revere, riding twice as long and securing enough volunteers to stave off the British, her name and story are mostly unknown. Then there's Shirley Chisholm, an educator from New York, who, in 1969, became the first African-American woman elected to Congress. And in 1972, she became the first major-party black candidate for President of the United States and the first woman to run for the Democratic presidential nomination.

Our journey through the history of the feminist movement brought up many more names that we had never heard before. It also brought up several important issues, such as pay equity, reproductive justice and equality. Based on the struggles and successes of the women who came before us, we—the young women of today—should feel as though we can achieve anything and be anything.

We drew on a quote from Nelson Mandela that serves as the driving inspiration for our program: "Sometimes it falls on a generation to be great. You can be that great generation. Let your greatness blossom."

There is much power in that quote. And the best way we know to use power for progress is to VOTE! There was a small problem though: high school girls aren't old enough to vote. So we decided that we were going to inspire people to take our issues into consideration when they voted. We brainstormed for a few hours and came up with an idea: we would create several posters that would be interwoven into a video along with other signs that read, "Vote for Me" and "Vote Like a Girl."

On a bright, sunny Sunday in September, the ambiance inside our classroom was very different than when we were originally talking about the history of feminism. This time, we were excited. We were inspired.

We brought together our friends, neighbors and family members to participate in the *Vote for Me* video. Each girl (from three to 17 years old) had the opportunity to make a poster that was reflective of an issue important to her. We stood holding our posters in various locations. The video was set to the song *Just a Girl* by the band No Doubt.

Below are some examples of the posters:

VOTE FOR ME:
★ "Because I have a dream"
★ "Because I'm worth it"
★ "So we can shatter the glass ceiling together"
★ "So I can grow up in a world without human trafficking"
★ "More than 120 nations provide paid maternity leave . . . the U.S. isn't one of them"
★ "Stand for my reproductive justice"
★ "Advocate for a healthy planet"
★ "Because the U.S. ranks 80th for elected women in national parliaments behind Lithuania (71), Afghanistan (37) and Cuba (2)"
★ "So I can be myself"
★ "Because one day I will vote for you"
★ "VOTE LIKE A GIRL!"

While a great success, the video was just the beginning. The women's movement needs to move. And so we are heeding the call to press forward. After all, if we don't create the future, someone else will.

Blossom Project posters

BECOME AN INFORMED CITIZEN
AND CREATE YOUR FUTURE!

The 2012 Blossom Project participants, under the guidance of Roweena Naidoo, are sending a strong message that now is the time to embrace who you are and to create your own future by becoming an informed citizen and taking positive actions to affect change. Learn more about history and the women and men who made it. In doing so, you will find new heroes to admire and learn from. Discover how you can become an informed citizen and let your voice be heard at BlossomProject.org and Fempowered.org.

CHAPTER EIGHT

 ## ROCK Your Passion!

Each one of us has been given
unique gifts in this life—
talents, interests and
opportunities—
and it is up to us
to use them to
rock the world.

Standing Up for Animals

by

Paul Shapiro

Looking back on my childhood, I might not have been the most likely candidate for someone who would choose to work full-time to prevent cruelty to animals. I was the kind of kid who always enjoyed a good joke, and more serious matters never really penetrated my mindset.

Some friends who had the misfortune of being in my chemistry class may remember me as the kid who would fill a beaker with water, loudly announce to be careful because I was coming through with hydrochloric acid, and then "clumsily" spill it all over an unwitting—and shrieking—victim's bare arm. This always delighted everyone who was in on the prank.

Even with my mind constantly thinking of increasingly elaborate pranks I could pull, just before I started high school, I began thinking about things that were a little more important. The first time I was exposed to the routine mistreatment of animals was when a friend showed me some films of animals confined on factory farms and being abused at slaughter plants, powerless in the face of their human tormentors who showed no mercy whatsoever. The animals were confined in cages so small they could barely move. They were mutilated without painkillers. They were electrocuted with prods to force them out onto the kill floor. Death was a relief for them.

I was horrified.

Having lived with dogs my whole life—which admittedly was only 13 years long at that point—I looked into the terrified eyes of the animals in the videos and saw my family dogs, struggling to free themselves from the cruelty that was obviously inescapable to any viewer. I imagined what I would have done to protect my dogs from such a fate, which of course was pretty much anything. And I demonized the people who I saw committing these acts of violence, at first thinking them to be sadists who must be stopped.

Of course, I quickly realized that much of the problem was not with the workers at factory farms—most of whom were simply doing their jobs—but with our society turning a blind eye to animal cruelty when the victims don't happen to be the kind of animals we deem worthy of our attention. In fact, as someone who indirectly financed these abuses every time I sat down to eat meat, I saw myself as more problematic for these animals than the people who were the immediate cause of their agony.

In order to help reduce animal suffering, I became vegetarian at age 13, and about a month later, after learning that the cruelty involved in the egg and dairy industries is often even worse than that of the meat industry, I became vegan. A year or so later, wanting to put my increasingly strong feelings about protecting animals into action, I formed a high school club called Compassion Over Killing.

Compassion Over Killing served free vegan meals during lunch to our classmates, brought in speakers, showed films and staged public educational events. Eventually, the group grew into a much larger organization than its humble beginnings as a high school club, raising enough money to hire several full-time staffers, myself included, and waging national campaigns.

We videotaped conditions at chicken and egg factory farms, livestock auctions, in transport trucks and in slaughter plants. Often, the footage would make its way onto the evening news or in the newspaper headlines. I hoped that our undercover exposés would lead to revelations and conversions similar to my own for those who ended up seeing them.

The goal of Compassion Over Killing was to shine a bright spotlight on the very dark world of factory farming and hope that the curative effect of such light would evaporate the abuse. We also challenged false animal welfare advertising claims made on the packaging of animal products and even brought an end to an egg industry-wide advertising scam.

After devoting much of my time to Compassion Over Killing over a span of 10 years (six as a volunteer and four as a full-time employee), I left to help start a farm animal protection campaign for The Humane Society of the United States (HSUS), the nation's largest animal protection organization.

Since joining HSUS, I've been fortunate to play a part in several efforts to improve the plight of farm animals. Most notably, we've succeeded in banning some of the most shocking factory farming practices in several states and worked with several retailers to help them stop buying products from the cruelest production systems. We've also helped make it more clear just how easy it is for individuals simply not to leave a trail of animal victims in the wake of our dietary choices.

But, despite the recent success that the U.S. animal movement has had battling cruelty to farm animals, their plight could still hardly be more dire. Billions of animals continue to be raised and killed in the United States each year, most in conditions that the vast majority of Americans would find simply appalling were they to actually bear witness to them. The longest journeys begin with single steps, and while we've taken some impressively important steps for animals in recent years, the task before us could still only be described as Herculean.

The vision we have is one in which our relationship with our fellow creatures is one that's no longer based on violence and domination, but rather is based upon compassion and respect. That vision—a truly humane society—may seem impossibly far away. But then again, every expansion of the circle of moral concern in our society at one point was viewed as little more than an unrealistic pipedream. The truth that these animals share the same spark of life that we do, that they suffer as we do, that they, too, want to live their lives, cannot be denied.

I may not have been the most likely candidate to become an animal advocate. But having now spent more than half of my first few decades campaigning for animals, it's clear to me that if someone like myself can play a role in helping move us closer to a truly humane society, certainly anyone is able to provide a voice for the voiceless, as well.

To every young person wondering if they have what it takes to become such a voice, the best advice I can offer is simply one sacred, all-important word: Start.

Inaction is the greatest opponent of social change. We can each start making the world a better place today, whether in our own lives with regard to what we eat, or in the rest of the world, too.

Maya Angelou put it better than I ever could: "Nothing will work unless you do."

Paul

START NOW!

Paul is the founder of Compassion Over Killing and vice president of Farm Animal Protection for The Humane Society of the United States. There is much power in Paul's one word call-to-action: START. Whatever dreams and goals you have, start right now to make them become a reality! Find out more about how you can start, or continue, to help animals by visiting COK.net (Compassion Over Killing) and HumaneSociety.org.

YOU Can
Make a Difference

by

Ashlee Kephart

It doesn't matter how old you are, YOU CAN MAKE A DIFFERENCE! I often hear people say, "I'm only one small person. What can I do?"

It only takes one smile, one encouragement, one hand, one listening ear, to give hope and value to another. You can take something you are passionate about—like music, gardening or books—and turn it into a program to serve others. I believe that everyone has something important to contribute; there is no contribution too small or insignificant. Service that can affect the whole world can start with a caring hello or opening a door, or giving a card, a pair of shoes, shelter, a song or simply your time. Volunteers giving of themselves through their time and talents bring societies together and unify humanity. By celebrating our differences and embracing our similarities, we not only become unique individuals, we also stay connected to one another.

That's why I founded Kids For A Better World, Inc., a nonprofit organization that encourages the empowerment of youth. For when we young people are encouraged to use our skills and talents in ways that serve others, we learn how to look beyond ourselves, to see the possibilities and to affect change. As a leader, I want to inspire and motivate others to see what is possible and get involved, to bring communities together and to enable individuals to live peaceful and productive lives. I believe volunteering is an important step in developing character and enriching society as a whole.

Opportunity is the key. The youth of today are facing a variety of challenges. Many are trapped in a cycle of violence, poverty and a lack of opportunities, all contributing to a sense of worthlessness and hopelessness for the future. They need opportunities to express themselves in positive ways and be given opportunities to lead, to be heard and to give service. These opportunities increase self-worth and by giving service, one becomes a productive member of society, focusing on what he or she can achieve, not on what he or she lacks.

Volunteering and giving service to others provides me the opportunities to make a difference and challenges my abilities and skills. When I'm helping others, I not only learn about them, I also learn more about myself. I learn to believe in myself and to see what's possible.

I started my first program at age nine. At age 16, I was a CEO of a nonprofit. Who I am today and what I have accomplished is directly related to the opportunities and encouragement I was given. This motivation is what carries me in wanting to help others realize their potential and to discover that they, too, can make a difference.

What are you passionate about?

Do you like to write? You can write thank you letters to our soldiers in harm's way, or write "I Care About You" cards for the homeless.

Do you like to draw? You can make holiday cards for nursing homes and veterans, or make Valentine's Day cards for Meals On Wheels recipients or patients in a children's hospital.

If you like to garden, you can participate in a community garden or help an African village raise food for their community by selling seeds. You can sell water bottles to raise money to build a well for a village in Africa. Anything you like to do can turn into a program to help others.

I love to read. So I took my love for reading and, at age nine, developed a program called "Books to Share Books To Read." This program distributes books, backpacks and school supplies to children's hospitals, third-world orphanages, neighborhood reading programs and shelters.

Another program I created is called "Walk In My Shoes." This program came about after visits to the organization Feed My Starving Children and seeing videos of the children and families with no shoes. I believe a good pair of shoes is important to one's health, so I started this program to provide shoes to underprivileged children and families, both locally and internationally.

Another program, "Caring Bags For The Homeless," is very dear to my heart. I started it in elementary school after a visit to a local shelter. Touring the facilities, I noticed an ice cream bucket in the corner of a makeshift shower filled with used community soap. It had a profound effect upon me. I started collecting trial size toiletries and placing them inside gallon-size Ziploc bags along with a washcloth, comb, bandages and, most importantly, a handmade card with the words "I CARE ABOUT YOU" on bright yellow cardstock.

After I made my first 100 bags, I was handing them out at a local shelter when an older gentleman came up to me with tears in his eyes and told me how much it meant to have something of his own. At that moment I knew this was not just a bag full of toiletry items—this was a bag full of hope.

Soon after, I enlisted family and friends and soon reached out to the community, peers, Girl Scouts, schools, churches, media, hotels and retail stores. The bags touched a core within every person who participated. When disasters happened across the country, I adapted the bags with items that would meet the needs of those communities. Soon, youth groups and churches got on board and now Caring Bags are given all across the country.

I have also found ways to incorporate my talents, skills, music and love for reading into programs that could make a difference. Along the way there were many challenges and barriers that presented themselves. Like when I wanted to play my violin at a local Ronald McDonald House, but was told I was too young to volunteer. Really?! I decided then and there that if I couldn't personally play for them, I would send the music in without me. I started a program called "Music from the Heart for Ronald McDonald House" and sent in music-related items so the kids could still experience the healing effects of the music.

I believe that obstacles are just steps of opportunities on the ladder of hope. When I see a need, I don't let barriers or even my age get in the way of providing a solution. My motto is: "Even if somebody tells you that something's impossible, that just means it hasn't been accomplished yet." While my age may have been seen as a barrier to others, I only saw the solutions. I feel that if you put your mind to it, you can accomplish anything.

Now, as I continue my education as a senior in college, my goal is to continue to empower youth by providing volunteer and educational opportunities and to spread the volunteer spirit internationally. Kids For A Better World, Inc. is supporting youth initiatives by going into the schools with our "Be the Change" service learning projects.

Giving someone an opportunity to make a difference has a domino effect. One kindness served upon another will create positive change. And positive outcomes, all building upon one another, benefit a community and bring societies together.

I believe caring is giving others opportunities, as opportunities are what change a life, and a changed life changes the world.

Ashlee

BE THE CHANGE!
Ashlee is the founder of Kids For A Better World where she chooses to be the change she wants to see in the world. And you can, too! Look beyond yourself and see who or what needs your assistance, and then lend your talents and skills to bring about positive change. Please visit KidsForABetterWorld.com.

Be a Boss—For Real!

by

Jack Kim

W hat's it like to be your own boss? Do you choose when and how long to work? Is it just the greatest thing ever?

Well, I'll tell you. It's extremely exciting and fun, but at times extremely stressful and time consuming. During the first year or so of running Benelab, my little web startup, I experienced so much of what I would have never learned sitting in a classroom. Also, I can safely say that while my venture has engulfed a huge part of my life, I have discovered a new, lifelong passion for social entrepreneurship.

Before I start rambling on about my organization and my experiences, I'd like to point out what it really is that I'm trying to get across to you with my story: I want to encourage young people to go out and start new things, build new things and do new things. There's nothing that will better provide you with experience and knowledge than going out and actually doing it. I hope the story of my experiences with Benelab will help make this point more clear.

A few years ago, when I was 16, I was on a plane heading home to Seattle. I had attended a three-week summer business camp held at Stanford University, which is just south of San Francisco. During my time there, I learned all sorts of different things about how companies operate and how to start my own business. The latter topic especially stood out to me because I was really into web development, branding, marketing and entrepreneurship.

After learning exactly how to start a company, I really wanted to go out and start my own to see what it was like. The only problem was that I had no idea what the company would do. I gave it some thought for a couple days, and then realized that I could scale up a current personal project—a nonprofit, charitable search engine—to target a bigger market and to create a bigger impact. And so I made up my mind to scale the website into a full-blown company and make it a nonprofit organization helping other nonprofits with the incredibly simple idea of donating ad revenue collected from web searches. I named the organization "Benelab" and set out to recruit about five of my diversely talented friends whom I wanted working on my startup. Within a week, I had a treasurer, a web developer, a graphic designer and a public relations manager on my team.

The next few months were filled with hard work and great rewards. Benelab proved to be very popular within my high school, and the school administrators even let us set the homepage of every computer in the school to Benelab.org. We got heavy press coverage, starting with a local online *Patch* article to national attention on Mashable.com. Media coverage was the only method we used to introduce Benelab to new people, and it worked out quite well.

Although we received a lot of attention for the idea behind creating a charitable search engine, the fact that the startup was run entirely by 16-year-old high schoolers proved to be more interesting to some people.

We partnered with Yahoo! to provide better search results and further monetize our web traffic. Last year, we worked 40-plus hours a week on a completely new division of Benelab, a division which allows any nonprofit organization to rebrand and launch its own crowd-sourced fundraising campaigns.

However, beyond the donation numbers and the volunteer numbers was the immeasurable experience the team was able to get. I, as chief executive officer, was able to learn how to manage people and keep a company innovating and motivated; McKayla, our vice president of marketing, was able to meet with dozens of other businesses and secure spots on national news and radio stations; Dalton, our web developer and chief technology officer, was able to gain experience building backend software for Benelab and learn how to work in a startup environment; and so on. We could have taken these types of classes in school, but I truly believe that the things we experienced with Benelab could not have been learned merely in a high school classroom setting.

A young age can sometimes be a disadvantage, but it can also be turned around and used as a huge advantage. Chances are, you have less to lose if you fail right now than if you fail 20 years from now, when you will actually have to feed yourself and have other major responsibilities. Basically, at an age like this, there really isn't much to lose, but there is much to gain.

Whatever your passion—whether it be business, engineering, singing or anything—there is always a way to go out and indulge yourself in real-world experiences. If it's business, start a company and make some money. If it's engineering, form a robotics team and compete in a world competition. If it's singing, start recording and go to auditions. Just do it. Take control of your passion and become a boss—literally.

So that's my story. I hope you were able to get a glimpse of how it's never too early to start something big, at any age.

Jack

GO OUT AND DO IT!
Jack is the founder and CEO of Benelab. His message is simple: Whatever it is you want to achieve in life, go out and do it! In his case, he combined his interest in starting an innovative search engine with a desire to help charitable causes. Start by asking yourself, *What goals in life do I have?* Then rock on from there! Check out more about how Jack realized his vision at Benelab.org.

One Word at a Time

by

<u>Kasey Dallman</u>

There are authors out there who say they would write even if they didn't have an audience. That they would write just because it's who they are. I used to agree with them. I used to think that was enough.

When I was 17 years old, my first young adult novel, *With the Flash of Lightning*, was published through an independent publisher. And I was stoked, so stoked that for the first few days after it was released, I traced my finger back and forth over the cover. At night, I slept with the book under my pillow to make sure the words never left my side. Crazy, I know.

But eventually, the publishing high began to wear off. Around that same time, a distant relative of mine passed away unexpectedly after a horrific car accident. The same accident left his younger sister fighting for her life in the hospital. I didn't really know the family at all, but their story consumed my thoughts. And I knew that I had to help them anyway I could.

I started spinning ideas around in my head. *How can I help?*

Eventually, I came to the conclusion that I wanted to donate money to the Children's Hospital of Wisconsin in Milwaukee to help the victim's younger sister. And I was going to raise this money through a percentage of royalties I earned from my book over a few months.

Alas, I took on the true joy that comes with writing. Words have always made me excited about life. Especially words that are woven and

---

crafted so carefully together that they create worlds far beyond our own.

I used to think that these words were only supposed to make me feel excited about life. But as soon as I donated part of my royalties to a heart-breaking cause, I saw that my words could also make everyone else excited.

Donating to the children's hospital was only the beginning. I still wrote because it was impossible not to. But I started writing for others to offer my readers nuggets of hope and humor and passion and inspiration with each turn of the page. And if my words weren't enough inspiration, I continued to comb through nonprofit organizations and donate royalties to charity after charity.

The charities I helped included a nonprofit foster group, because my novel focuses on a damaged foster child trying to find a sense of family. Another was the American Lung Cancer Association, in memory of my grandmother who passed away from the disease all too soon. And, the Lewy Body Dementia Association, a charity nominated by one of my readers. My latest venture has me donating 100 percent of my royalties to a company that provides music lessons to foster children. I can't wait to make out that check!

Ever since my novel was published in 2009, I have been giving away a cut of my royalties. And if book sales are down and my royalties aren't high enough, I add more of my own money.

Every kid out there has something that he or she excels in, something that they can use to inspire or help others. And mine is writing. The world took a chance on me when it allowed me to become a writer. So I give back to the world. One dollar at a time. One word at a time.

Kasey and her book

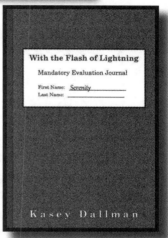

With the Flash of Lightning

Mandatory Evaluation Journal

First Name: Serenity
Last Name: _____

Kasey Dallman

USE WHAT YOU'VE GOT!

Kasey is a reporter for *Amazing Kids! Magazine*. Like Kasey says, everyone has talents and skills—the key is to discover what you're good at and then use those gifts to help a cause that is important to you. Read all about young people who are rocking the planet with their talents and good works at Amazing-Kids.org.

Social Justice for All!

by

Samantha Huffman

Growing up, Special Olympics was always a part of my life. In second grade, one of my friends asked me if I wanted to help out in a special education classroom once a week during recess. I agreed and assisted the students with their math assignments or coloring a picture. Or I would read a book or play a game with them. Throughout the year, I started going more and more until eventually I was giving up all of my recesses to be in the special education classroom every day.

People always asked me why I did it, and I didn't really have an answer. I was only seven years old. Before this, I had no connection to the disability population and, at the time, I didn't really understand the depth of what I was doing. I just knew that I loved being there and that these students were my friends. The next year, when I turned eight years old, I was asked to become a Unified Partner for Special Olympics. A Unified Partner is someone without an intellectual disability who plays on a sports team with athletes who have intellectual disabilities. I jumped at the chance to become a Unified Partner.

I continue to be a Unified Partner to this day. But when I was a senior in high school, I was offered another opportunity—I was selected to be a member of the National Youth Activation Committee for Special Olympics Project UNIFY. Project UNIFY is a youth-led organization that educates, motivates and activates youth to create inclusion in schools and communities through both sports and education. I was immediately drawn into the work they were doing.

In the summer after my freshman year in college, we held a National Youth Activation Summit for 200 young people, with and without intellectual disabilities, from across the country. The purpose of our summit was to focus on our goal of social justice and how we could use Special Olympics as a platform to achieve this goal.

To prepare for the summit, a year earlier I was assigned the job of being the chair for the sessions committee, which created and led all of the sessions for the summit. The summer of the summit, I was also given the opportunity to be an intern for Special Olympics Project UNIFY at the Special Olympics International headquarters in Washington, D.C. There, I helped organize and lead the entire summit, which included scheduling, collaborations and logistics.

The preparation for the summit had me working with many education leaders from across the country, including Charles Haynes, a First Amendment scholar and social justice expert. Until that summer, I hadn't realized what my work with Special Olympics really was, but now I did: I was fighting for social justice and social change for those with intellectual disabilities. I discovered that social justice was my passion. And, I realized that fighting for social justice was my specialty.

I originally went to college to major in elementary education, but during my senior year, I realized that my goal in life had changed. I decided to apply to graduate school for a master's degree in social work with a concentration on social change.

Whether it is with Special Olympics or another like-minded organization, one thing is for certain: because of experiences going all the way back to when I was seven years old, I am now here to stay in the disability movement. My fight for social justice isn't going to stop with being a Unified Partner or a member of the Special Olympics family. It is my passion. It is my career. It is my life.

Samantha with Jared Niemeyer

TURN YOUR PASSION INTO A CAREER!

Samantha is a Unified Partner for Special Olympics and a former member of the National Youth Activation Committee for Special Olympics Project UNIFY. Like Samantha, you can turn your volunteer work into a career by studying areas like social work, special education and other topics, and then someday pursuing jobs in those areas. Learn more about volunteer and job opportunities with Special Olympics by visiting SpecialOlympics.org and R-word.org (R-word: Spread the Word to End the Word).

My SWT Life

by

Syreeta Gates

As I reflect on my journey to this point in my life, who would have thought that my love for Polo Ralph Lauren clothes would be, as author Malcolm Gladwell calls it, the "tipping point?" On my quest to get "fly," I saw some young black and brown people on Polo.com who looked like me, which is something that doesn't happen very often. So I jumped at the chance and found out more.

I was only 17 years old. I called the Polo Ralph Lauren corporate offices. I wasn't just randomly calling Fortune 500 companies—I now had a mission. My goal was to be down with whatever or whoever got those young people on that site, period. I was connected to Polo.com, and then to the Corporate Responsibility department, who then gave me the number for Divine Bradley, the founder of Team Revolution.

Little did I know that Divine, too, was a collector of the Polo brand and had created a partnership between Team Revolution and the Polo Fashion School. I finally dialed his number, secretly praying he wouldn't pick up. But when he did, I knew I had to sell him the dream . . . whatever I decided it was.

Long story short, I became a part of Divine's Fellowship Academy and part of the Polo Fashion School program. At the end of the Fellowship Academy, we students had to decide to be one of three things: an expansion leader, program director or social entrepreneur. This was the first time I had ever heard the term "social entrepreneur." I had had prior sales experience like selling popcorn, bookmarks, clothes and also making home-baked cakes, so I had no doubt in my mind that I was going to head in the social entrepreneur direction.

But then I thought, *Where on earth do I start?* I had been throwing teen parties around that time, so I thought maybe creating a teen lounge would be cool. Another idea I had was to open a store and call it "The Gift Shop." This store would sell products associated with organizations that do amazing work, and then the organizations would receive a percentage of the proceeds.

After many long months trying to figure it out and doing tons of service projects like murals with a brilliant graffiti artist and holding a hip-hop conference I created with Life Camp Inc., I decided on creating The SWT Life. SWT is an acronym for "Service We Trust" and its original purpose was to do cool community service projects that my friends and I would be interested in.

I felt the problem was that among young people the concept of service had a negative undertone to it. In their worlds, community service had to be done for three reasons: 1) You needed it to meet a school requirement; 2) Someone told you it would look good on your resume for college; or 3) You got into some legal trouble and were forced to do it.

It helped that Jay Z had a song titled *Sweet* on his latest record at that time, which sealed the deal for the name. My goal was to transform the way community service projects were done. I wanted to make service the flyest thing on the planet. As I got older and gained more experience running programs, facilitating workshops, doing speaking engagements and participating in more service projects, I began to realize that I was on the quest for my true purpose.

Eventually, I discovered what I was passionate about through trial and error. While working on numerous programs and throwing myself into various experiences, it became clear what I liked and didn't like. It was clear that I wanted to give more rather than give back, and to me there was a major difference. To me, giving back was simply volunteering at an organization with no profound connection to it, but giving MORE requires a passion for what you are doing.

Because I am passionate about hip-hop and history, giving MORE would include, for example, creating a documentary on hip-hop to inspire young people to become historians. It's a direct reflection of who I am. Once I got hip to giving more, my purpose changed and so did The SWT Life. I went from doing community service projects to helping young people find their superpower.

Throughout these past years, I've also been searching for answers to certain questions: What are my strengths? What am I passionate about? What is my purpose? I feel that if you know the answers to these three questions, you can move through the world with swag. You're simply unstoppable like X-Men, Power Rangers, the kids in the cartoon *Recess* or [insert your favorite super group here].

Since answering those questions for myself, I've had a new quest: assisting young people who are becoming SWT lifers to find their passions, purposes and strengths through a series of conversations and activities. SWT lifers attend principle-based workshops like Lifestyle Design, which allows them to re-imagine their roles in the world; The Blueprint, which is an introduction to life coaches and astrologers; and Impact Making, which helps them create a passion project. The SWT lifers also complete a 30-day project implementation with the help of dynamic people, including powerhouses like Apple. This combination of experiences has led to the evolution of not only my own superpower, but also for many other young people on similar quests.

While I'm committed to being a rock star and a role model in this life and in the causes I believe in, I challenge you to find your superpower, to re-imagine the world as you see it, and to continue to live The SWT Life.

Syreeta

GIVE MORE!

Syreeta is the founder of The SWT Life and Just BE Cause. Take up her challenge to go above and beyond the call of duty and give more of yourself—use your superpowers of talent and skills to push the limits of what's possible. Find out how Syreeta is pushing past limits by visiting TheSWTLife.com, SyreetaGates.com and JustBECauseBook.com.

CHAPTER NINE

Heal the World

The power to heal the world begins
with each one of us and is as
simple as picking up a paintbrush,
reaching out a helping hand,
kicking a soccer ball
or asking a question.

The Unity Mural

by

Nada Abdallah

Assalamu alaikum, Peace be upon you!
I am a volunteer at Arab American Family Services (AAFS) where we are working on a very exciting new project. For the project, my fellow teenage (and younger) partners and I are painting a mural that will be displayed at the AAFS headquarters in Chicago. The mural represents togetherness and the message that you will never be alone in the world.

The purpose of this project is to show how we are all connected to each other. It will also represent that whoever comes to AAFS will be well taken care of and helped with whatever they need. That is important to remember because when people come to AFFS seeking help they will be looking at this extraordinary mural, and hopefully they will feel safe and welcomed.

For the mural, we are painting the world in space. Around the image of the world, we will paint many symbolic monuments representing various countries, such as Lady Liberty, the Egyptian pyramids, the Eiffel Tower, the Lotus Temple, the Taj Mahal of Agra and the Leaning Tower of Pisa. There will also be a huge, painted banner saying, "Welcome to AAFS" and much more.

This project has been an amazing experience so far. I'm having a lot of fun, but I also have had some challenging moments. The fun part is meeting new people, painting and, most importantly, helping the community. The most challenging part as a group was deciding what we should draw on the mural and if people will like it and understand it.

This project will demonstrate unity and togetherness, which will be shown by all the diverse monuments and how they are all on top of the world. That will show that unity is very important in our daily life. You may be wondering why is it we picked unity as a theme. We thought that this topic was very important to the current state of the world. Today, everybody is at war or in the midst of other conflicts with each other. We would like for the people who come to AAFS to look at this extraordinary mural and think about it deeply.

How did I end up working on this project and meeting wonderful people? That goes back to how I got involved in the first place. I did this project at first because I needed community service hours for school. I have to admit to that because it started off as nothing more than community service hours, but now it's so much more than that. To tell you the truth, I am fully done with my community service hours. Now I am working on the mural because I am dedicated and willing to put my effort into this magnificent project that we have been working on for a long time.

AAFS means a lot to me. It is my second home. It's where I can really express myself through activities like working on the mural. I'm so happy that I got involved in this project. It really means a lot to me, and I can't wait to see how well it will turn out. I don't have a special job. I just paint and brainstorm with my partners. I wouldn't say that I am an awesome painter or drawer. Actually, I suck at drawing, but I love mixing colors and painting. Plus, I have learned a lot from our supervisors, Hamza and Sara, not only about painting, but also about working together.

I think it's important that teens get involved in art because art is how people can connect with themselves and other people. You may think that art isn't very important, or that it can't help people connect with each other. All those people who think that are WRONG! That's what art is for!

Teens should get involved in art because art is fun and because, in addition to talking about issues and concerns, art is also a great way to express feelings! The mural has truly been a pleasant and inspiring experience for me and my new friends. I have learned a lot of things, but the most important thing that I have learned is that no matter how young you are, you can still help the world and even change it for the better.

Nada

CREATE UNITY!

Nada is an advocate for Arab American Family Services. Just like Nada and her friends, you can create unity in many ways, whether at school or in your community. Start a club, gather a few friends together to work on a charity project, create your own unity mural or become active in something else that brings people together for a common purpose. Please visit ArabAmericanFamilyServices.org to learn more.

Changing the World, Heart to Heart

by

Ana Dodson

I was born in Cusco, Peru and my parents adopted me when I was a baby and brought me to the United States. During the summer of 2003, when I was 11 years old, my mother and I went to Peru to visit orphanages. I took children's books written in Spanish and teddy bears that I had collected for the children.

The Hogar Mercedes de Jesus Molina is a small orphanage in Anta, which is located in the hills outside of Cusco. I really wanted to visit the Hogar since it is near where I was born. When we went to the Hogar and had given the children the books and teddy bears, we discovered that the orphanage had never had visitors before!

As my mother and I prepared to leave, one girl named Yenivel, whom I had gotten to know, hugged me and started to cry. She said, "Ana, I know you will not forget us and that one day you will help."

When I was a baby I could have been put in an orphanage, and into that same situation. Yenivel's unforgettable words really moved and inspired me to do something more to help.

I have so many things in my life that I tend to take for granted. I have wonderful loving parents who support me in any way they can and I have a wonderful education. My visit to the orphanage made me realize that I wanted those girls to have what I have. I also realized that they needed more than books and teddy bears. I believed that if I tried, I might be able to really help them.

When I formed Peruvian Hearts, my goal was to give the girls a better education and improve their quality of life. Peruvian Hearts now provides all the basic needs for the 27 girls living at the Hogar. This includes food, medical, dental and psychological services. The girls attend private schools where they can get a better quality of education and they have access to daily academic tutoring at the orphanage. We also created a computer lab where they attend computer classes in addition to English classes.

The other changes at the Hogar were equally dramatic and impactful. Meals used to be served on a partially enclosed patio that served as a dining room. The kitchen was a small, poorly ventilated room with a large clay wood-burning stove. In fact, many of the girls had eye infections because of the lack of ventilation for the smoke. Ducks roamed freely throughout the dining room, and rain and wind often made mealtime in the small kitchen impossible.

With the generous support of various organizations and donors, we were able to build a modern kitchen and large airy dining room, which has become the heart of the orphanage. That, plus the addition of modern bathrooms with warm and clean water, all contributed to an environment of dignity and health for the children.

In addition to supporting the girls at the Hogar, Peruvian Hearts also provides lunch and a multi-vitamin to hundreds of children daily. These children walk for two hours to and from school and now have the nutrition they need to enable them to pay attention and learn more effectively. Education is one of the most critical elements to breaking the cycle of poverty, but without food it is hard to take advantage of one's education.

The approach we believe in at Peruvian Hearts is to go deeper rather than wider. In the summer of 2011, Peruvian Hearts launched a new program called Peruvian Promise, which has been my dream for many years. We finally saw it come to fruition. I believe this program will help us move from merely enhancing the lives of the girls with whom we work to actually giving them the tools they need to transform their lives and empower them to transform the lives of their families.

The Peruvian Promise program focuses on the development of greater self-esteem in addition to mentorship opportunities and service to others. In addition, each girl is provided with a high quality secondary education, and then the chance to attend university or post-secondary vocational education. This will then give her the chance for employment and a life of dignity.

Each girl treasures the opportunity to become a professional, which will enable her to give educational support to her siblings and to help provide her family with the resources to live in dignity. The girls have expressed interest in studying areas such as civil engineering, medicine, nursing, accounting, tourism and hotel management, cosmetology and law.

Peruvian Hearts has a secondary mission, which is to inspire young people to get involved in service and philanthropy. I love having the opportunity to speak to groups of youth to help them understand that they don't have to wait to be adults to begin to affect change in the world. I believe that each person can change the world a little bit at a time.

My experience since I founded Peruvian Hearts has been profound and a defining force in my life. It has taught me so many things, but one of the most important lessons is that even when one sees a situation that appears to be helpless, there is still hope. I know I can't change the world in a day, and I know I can't do it by myself, but I believe that people working together really can make a difference.

Mother Teresa once said, "If you can't feed a hundred people, feed just one." These words have guided my work. They have helped me to understand that making a small difference is still important. When many people each make a small difference, the ripples of those acts create a world that is bright with the light those individual acts have brought with them.

Ana and a friend

SMALL DIFFERENCES HAVE BIG IMPACTS!

Ana is the founder of Peruvian Hearts where small differences and subtle acts of compassion have a huge impact in the lives of young people every day. You can think BIG by acting small and taking nothing for granted—the road to helping others and to achieving your goals begins with a tiny step forward. Take a step forward by visiting PeruvianHearts.org.

When Strangers Become Family

by

Hannah Katz

Ilike to think that there are three categories of people in my life: strangers, friends and family. Yet somehow, somewhere along my trip to a rural Zimbabwean village, the lines separating the three merged. Every stranger I met was a friend, and every friend I made became family.

I was nine years old when my dad got involved with his friend Mark Grashow's charity—the U.S.-Africa Children's Fellowship. The charity did many things, including donating books and school supplies to a distant African country. At that point, all I had ever changed was my hair into a ponytail. I had not changed another life. However, when my family was offered the opportunity to travel halfway around the world to tour the country of Zimbabwe, which is north of South Africa, and to also help out in their schools, I jumped in with no hesitation whatsoever.

I honestly had no idea of what to expect from the trip. I kept a journal along the way. On the plane ride to South Africa, I wrote: "I'm scared to see what these people's lives are like, and that I won't be able to help ..."

I knew vaguely of what I was getting into. What I didn't know was how some people there didn't need changing. They were some of the most proud and hospitable human beings I've ever met.

After touring Zimbabwe and going on safaris, my family and I traveled to the Swazi District, a rural village over an hour away from the city of Bulawayo. With a friend of Mark's as our outstanding interpreter and guide, we stayed in the ORAP center located in Swazi. ORAP, which stands for "Organization of Rural Associations for Progress," is a nonprofit organization that works with Mark's charity to help send books, supplies and clothes to small communities of people. This inspiring organization has branches that provide health care, AIDS medicine, food, education and jobs for the Zimbabwean people.

Organizations like ORAP completely amaze me. It's incredible how even in a country ravished by poverty and misfortune, there are still selfless individuals making the world a better place. I continue to be inspired by them, and am thankful to be reminded that there is still good in the world.

At the ORAP center, our housing consisted of cement walls, single beds with mattresses, a lack of electricity, two toilets without toilet seats, two shower stalls that no longer sported the luxury of running water and an intricately woven thatched roof that let in plenty of cold air. I'm not complaining, only emphasizing how much nicer this was than the average village hut, or even their school. For example, the school bathrooms were cement outhouses with no ventilation, and the toilets were basically just holes in the ground. This lack of sanitation in rural communities is a huge factor of childhood sickness in Zimbabwe.

Even though the buildings weren't ideal, every school that we visited welcomed us with open arms, mouths and lots of food! After being introduced to the students at every school, a glee club would sing their local songs and dance with us. They would stomp their feet and laugh hysterically at us when we tried to imitate them. It's crazy to think that even across the world these kids, who had basically nothing, were the same as the kids back home. They loved to sing loud and danced without a care in the world.

Not only were we welcomed with song, but also with food. Every new friend I met wanted to feed me. The ORAP center provided a huge breakfast every morning for us, followed by a filling 10 o'clock tea (with sandwiches, of course!), lunch at noon, and then a giant dinner in the evening.

At one of the primary schools, my mom and I visited the teachers' houses (more like rooms) on the school property. One particularly generous teacher wanted to give us corn that they had cooked. We accepted, but with quiet regrets, because we realized that the corn was probably their entire dinner for that night. Not only did the corn taste like candle wax, but the teacher then insisted that we take the whole bag! In Zimbabwean culture, it would have been worse not to accept their gift than to take their meal for that evening. When we returned to the ORAP center, workers gratefully accepted our re-gifted corn.

In between the touring and eating, my 16-year-old sister and I tested the eyesight of several teachers and older students to see if they needed glasses. We are currently in the process of sending glasses to those who needed them. Besides performing eye exams, I made friendship bracelets with older students, played matching games with the younger kids and got a true taste of the Zimbabwean lifestyle. Surprisingly I envied their simplistic lifestyle, where dreams are just dreams, New York City is on another planet and varsity soccer consists of intense games on a dirt field (with cleats, if you're lucky!).

On my last day in the Swazi district, our whole group visited a primary school by means of local transportation called a "scotch cart." We arrived at the school after an hour of bouncing along in the cart; because the cart was pulled by two unlucky donkeys, getting there safely was a miracle all in itself! However, when we arrived, all of the little kids were singing a song that we had become familiar with throughout our trip. "We are together (we are together oh' lord) we are a family—we love each other. We love each other (we love each other oh' lord) we are a family."

It was one of the most emotional moments of the whole experience for me, because I realized that even though I couldn't fix every student, child or human being there, I was still part of their family. I think the Zimbabwean people might just have the definition of family correct—family is more than just sharing the same blood. Family in Zimbabwe is your neighbor, your stray dog, your harvest god. Family is your priest, your wool hat, your brand new textbook. And best of all, their family now includes me. I'm still not sure that I came back from the trip a completely changed person, but I hope that the place I came back from changed because of me.

Hannah with four of her new friends in Zimbabwe.

CHOOSE TO USE NEW EXPERIENCES!

Hannah is an advocate for Kids Helping Kids Connecticut. Just like Hannah did on her trip, embrace the unexpected things and interactions that come your way every day—the new people you meet, the new experiences you hadn't planned on, the new gifts you never asked for—and use those relationships and newfound knowledge for good works. Please visit KidsHelpingKidsCT.org and TheChildrensFellowship.org.

What's in Your Water?

by

<u>Jordyn Schara</u>

What would you do if you discovered that your community's drinking water contained traces of someone else's birth control medicine or heart medicine? Or even antibiotics?

I found this to be the case here in Wisconsin where I live, and I did something about it.

Before I tell you my story, here are some facts I discovered during my research:

★ The U.S. Geological Survey tested 139 streams across the U.S. and found and documented levels of prescription drugs and hormones in that water.

★ According to an Associated Press investigation, a concoction of drugs—including antibiotics, anti-convulsants, acne medication, mood stabilizers and sex hormones—have been found in the drinking water supplies of at least 41 million Americans. This investigation reviewed hundreds of scientific reports, analyzed federal drinking water databases, visited environmental study sites and treatment plants, and interviewed more than 230 officials, academics and scientists.

★ Even though our planet is 70 percent water, only an astonishing 1.5 percent is fresh water, used for human and animal consumption. This water is now being contaminated by prescription and over-the-counter drugs whenever anyone disposes of medication in a toilet, down a sink or in the trash. The Environmental Protection Agency (EPA) has clearly stated that sewage treatment systems are not specifically engineered to remove pharmaceuticals.

★ The federal government doesn't require any testing and hasn't set safety limits for drugs in water. Even users of bottled water and home filtration systems are exposed. Some bottlers simply repackage tap water and do not typically treat or test for pharmaceuticals. The same goes for the makers of home filtration systems.

★ Contamination is not confined to the United States. More than 100 different drugs have been detected in waterways throughout the world. Fish and prawns in China exposed to untreated wastewater had shortened life spans. And in Norway, Atlantic salmon exposed to estrogen in the North Sea had severe reproductive problems.

★ Because of all of this, recent studies have found alarming effects, for both humans and wildlife, when it comes to wastewater not being treated for medications. For humans, small amounts of medication exposure have caused human breast cancer cells to grow faster, kidney cells to grow too slowly and blood cells to show signs of inflammation. An example of the effects on wildlife has occurred in fish: Male fish are being feminized and female fish have developed male genitalia organs.

Even though scientists are researching the extent of this contamination, our government is hurting us by not proactively addressing the problem. I decided to meet this challenge head on by spreading awareness and providing communities with a safe way to dispose of these toxic drugs. I founded the Wisconsin Prescription Pill and Drug Disposal (WI P2D2) program. WI P2D2 is a teen-organized drug collection program dedicated to keeping the water systems of the world safe from the irreversible damage caused by the improper disposal of medication.

Before I started WI P2D2, consumers were being told by pharmacies, doctors and the U.S. government to dispose of their medications by pouring them down the drain, flushing them in the toilet or throwing them out in the trash. All of these methods are seriously detrimental to our environment.

My desired outcome for WI P2D2 is twofold: 1) To educate the world that improper disposal of drugs contaminates our ground water, which results in deformities in amphibians and unknown genetic problems to humans, and 2) To provide communities with a safe means to dispose of their drugs. Since our state and federal governments were not even acknowledging that this danger existed, let alone trying to address it by providing us with secure disposal options, the impact on our local area was significant.

But then I discovered an even more urgent reason to create WI P2D2—our family medicine cabinets are now the new drug dealers. The prescription drugs and over-the-counter medicines parents and adults leave unsecured in medicine cabinets are fueling the newest drug problem among America's teens: prescription and over-the-counter drug abuse. Studies have found that more people—mostly teens—abuse prescription drugs than cocaine, heroin and methamphetamine combined. Recognizing this important nationwide issue made me more driven to find a way to properly dispose of all medication and prescription drugs.

When launching WI P2D2, I contacted the Drug Enforcement Agency, the Department of Natural Resources, the EPA and the Department of Justice. None of these governmental agencies was willing to tackle this insidious problem or help me with my project. So I started in my hometown and laid the groundwork for creating a drug collection program. This was a monumental task, considering it is illegal to collect or accept prescription drugs from anyone. Plus, the cost to dispose of these drugs properly is too expensive.

Once I worked out the details of my program, I contacted my local police chief and made a presentation to our city council. When I was done, they gave me a standing ovation and even provided me with funds to start my program. At that point, I made presentations to the local hospital, pharmacists, civic organizations, business leaders and schools to recruit volunteers and spread awareness.

I then launched a marketing campaign by creating my own brochures and flyers and distributing them around town. I made posters, had banners designed and created funny and engaging designs for T-shirts. But the most unique and interesting way I promoted WI P2D2 was by creating a mascot named "Phil the Pill Bottle." Needless to say, Phil was an instant hit!

WI P2D2 was growing quickly and I needed more money. I looked at many options, but decided a grant would be best because it was free money—WI P2D2 would not have to pay it back. I am proud to say that I became the first teen organization to have written and been awarded a Wisconsin state drug grant! The financial help was just what WI P2D2 needed to carry on its important mission.

So far, we have held multiple drug collection events, started programs in many Wisconsin communities, hosted both a free needle/sharps disposal program and a free mercury thermometer swap, and have helped keep more than 900,000 pounds of drugs out of our groundwater. We have purchased several drug drop-off boxes for communities, enlisting high school student volunteers to paint and decorate these containers. WI P2D2 has also helped cities purchase incinerators, thus saving taxpayer dollars on medication disposal costs, mentored teens and adults across the country with their programs, and has become a national model for teen-created drug collection programs. WI P2D2 has even joined forces with a dynamic science teacher/mentor from Illinois, who already had his own drug collection program.

As of this writing, WI P2D2 has spread across the country and can be found in more than 22 states. What started out as curiosity on my part has blossomed into the largest teen-run, self-sustainable drug collection program in the world!

So I ask you again: What's in your water?

Jordyn

HAVE YOUR WISHES GRANTED!

Jordyn is the founder of Wisconsin Prescription Pill and Drug Disposal Program (WI P2D2). Take a cue from Jordyn when it comes to funding your charity project and apply for grants. A grant is money awarded by government agencies and non-profit organizations to individuals and organizations for all or part of worthy projects. Take the time to research and apply for grants related to your project. There's nothing to lose and lots to gain! Learn more about Jordyn's many projects at HelpingOurPeersExcel.com.

Alive and Kicking

by

David Kapata

Originally I was a Grassroot Soccer (GRS) coach in Lusaka, the capital and largest city in Zambia. But I have now taken on the new role as program coordinator for Grassroot Soccer Zambia. In this role, I work for GRS, which is a nonprofit organization, educating young people in my community here in Africa and in other places about HIV and AIDS prevention, and how to live a healthy life using soccer-based activities. Through this experience, I have been privileged to gain a lot of valuable insight, which has been instrumental in defining my outlook on life's challenges.

My mother died when I was nine years old, and the months leading up to her death took a huge emotional, psychological and financial toll on my family and me. Though I was too young to fully understand that she was suffering from an AIDS-related illness, I knew right then that when given a chance, I would do anything to prevent other people from going through what my mother had gone through.

Seven years after my mothers' death, my younger sister, who was only seven years old, also died from an AIDS-related illness. My sister's untimely death left me with a lot of unresolved questions, which caused me to become very bitter because I couldn't understand why AIDS would affect someone so young and defenseless.

My introduction to the work of GRS came as a twist of fate. Eventually, it became a way for me to help stop HIV and AIDS by inspiring and empowering young people.

I had always been a very athletic student and enjoyed anything that gave me a chance to participate in outdoor activities. Therefore, the first time I got to experience a GRS program, I knew I had to get involved. I was so inspired by the dynamic and energetic coaches that right then and there, I knew I wanted to be just like them.

After I graduated, the coaches encouraged me to join a GRS peer-education group at a community youth center in Chilenje Township. It was there that I was trained as a Skillz Coach. The Skillz curriculum teaches basic life skills that help boys and girls to adopt healthy behaviors and live risk free. Being a coach was not only a great forum for me to openly face my own fears about HIV and AIDS, but also to develop my personal efficacy.

The past six years with GRS have challenged me to move beyond my comfort zone, and as a result I have been fortunate to accomplish a lot of my professional goals. Nonetheless, the biggest turning point for me came when I was invited to facilitate at a retreat for HIV-positive children. Going into the retreat, I was very nervous. Looking at the children reminded me so much of my younger sister. I couldn't help but think about whether she would have suffered the same fate had she had the opportunity to learn about how to protect herself, and perhaps even live with her AIDS-related disease.

However, I have come to realize that the experiences I went through with my sister's death now give me the ability to relate to and comfort children who are going through the same situation. I have come to accept that HIV and AIDS are a part of my everyday life, and therefore I choose to take a stance and make a difference in my community, instead of becoming a victim of fear.

Working for GRS never fails to challenge my skills or test my resolve. It's where I can lead with confidence and guide with my heart, and it's a place where I always feel I can make a difference. The work I am able to do with GRS allows me the opportunity to do everything I love doing, while also making a positive difference in the lives of young people in my community.

Working under the Spaces for Sport project has especially exposed me to a new perspective on life. There is an amazing partnership between Barclays Bank and GRS here in Lusaka called "Skillz for Youth," which is bringing together 100 young adult community role models, 16,000 youth program participants and up to 100,000 community members. Because of my commitment to GRS's mission, I was honored with the opportunity to first become the assistant program coordinator for the Barclay Spaces for Sport project and now the program coordinator.

As a result of my experiences with Grassroot Soccer, I have become more focused, determined and dedicated in every aspect of my life. I now hope that my story can inspire other young people to take up a challenge that they are passionate about and make a difference in their own communities.

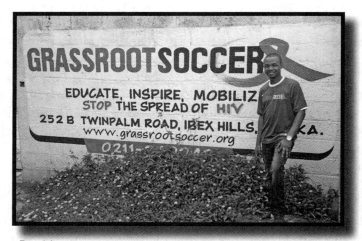

David

TURN TRAGEDY INTO TRIUMPH!

David is the program coordinator for Grassroot Soccer Zambia. When tragedy strikes, as it did to David's family, find a way to learn from it and make good come of it. Just like David is now helping to educate thousands of young people, you, too, can use the tragedies and challenges in your life to ultimately better yourself and the lives of others. Please visit GrassrootSoccer.org.

Fixing Broken Hearts

by

<u>Sarah Kladar</u>

It is a Kladar family tradition not to receive actual birthday gifts from our friends. Instead, my siblings—Emily, Thomas, Will and Ellie—and I ask friends to donate to a charity of our choosing.

Up until age five, we have friends bring food for the local food bank. After we turn five, it is up to us to decide how we will help others. For example, in the past I have collected money for breast cancer research, my sister collected books for the devastated libraries in New Orleans after Hurricane Katrina, and together we have gathered school supplies for needy children.

Around my eighth birthday, we decided to all work toward one charity, a charity of our own creation—Kids Helping Kids Fix Broken Hearts. The charity was founded in 2008. But I'm getting ahead of myself. Let me explain how this all started.

During a family trip to Mexico, we were invited to visit a small medical clinic in a very poor part of Playa del Carmen. Inside the clinic was a wall of children's photos. We inquired as to the purpose of the photos and learned they were images of local children who would die without heart surgery because of a lack of funds. We felt desperate to do something. They were kids just like us. We couldn't imagine what it must feel like to be them. Little did we know that this visit would turn into a life-changing experience for all of us.

When we returned home, we decided we needed to make a difference in those children's lives. We started walking dogs and selling lemonade to accumulate funds for heart surgeries. When these tasks weren't bringing in enough money to help the children, we decided on a bigger project—to sell something practical, yet cheap to purchase.

That's when we decided to start Kids Helping Kids Fix Broken Hearts. Emily, being the artist of the family, drew a logo for the project, and I was the one to name the charity. We discussed printing the logo on T-shirts (too common) or on coffee mugs (too expensive). After brainstorming, we came up with the idea of dishtowels, and then had Emily's hand-drawn logo screen-printed onto them.

We started selling our dishtowels for $5 each. At first, we ordered 50 dishtowels, thinking we would send $250 back to the clinic. The dishtowels sold quickly, so we ordered more. When our local hospital heard what we were doing, we were invited to sell our dishtowels at an annual Christmas event. In one weekend, we sold 650 of them!

A few months later, we were invited to speak at a church. We sold 850 dishtowels and made more than $4,000! That same weekend, complete strangers offered to build us a website. We were then invited to more local civic groups to talk about Kids Helping Kids Fix Broken Hearts. In six months, we had raised $15,000 dollars.

We returned to Mexico to pay for procedures for 13 young kids. When we arrived, we were not prepared for the hundred or more people who had gathered to see us present the money. The highlight of the day was meeting the children whose lives we were going to help save. Their gratitude made our hearts overflow with joy!

When we returned to the United States, we thought our project was over. We were very wrong. After a series of events, we decided it would be better to move Kids Helping Kids Fix Broken Hearts from serving only Mexico to the United States, deciding to help children in our own country, too. By word of mouth, our charity kept growing. Soon, partnerships were created with hospitals to reach families from around the country.

Currently, we are partners with Johns Hopkins Children's Hospital in Baltimore, Texas Children's Hospital in Houston, St. Louis Children's Hospital in St. Louis and Sacred Heart Hospital in Spokane. Since partnering with these hospitals, we have helped 18 children from 11 states and one child from Costa Rica.

In 2011, I was a national winner of a $10,000 college scholarship from Kohl's Department store and their amazing "Kohl's Cares for Kids" program. The same year, our charity was a top 10 finalist for the 2011 Small Charity of the Year Award at the Classy Awards in San Diego. In May of 2012, my sister, Emily, was a National Prudential Spirit of Community Award winner and named one of America's Top 10 Youth Volunteers for 2012 in Washington, D.C.

As of this writing, we have sold more than 6,200 dishtowels and raised almost $80,000. And we have at least one dishtowel in all 50 states and in 36 countries. Our goal is to help at least one child from all 50 states. We are well on our way thanks to many caring people around the world.

No one is ever too young to make a difference. You just have to have enough courage to use the opportunities presented to you.

Top row: Will and Sarah; bottom row: Emily, Ellie and Thomas

IT'S BETTER TO GIVE THAN TO RECEIVE!

Sarah is the co-founder of Kids Helping Kids Fix Broken Hearts. Like the Kladars, turn your next birthday into a charity event. Instead of gifts, ask your family and friends to donate money to your favorite charity, or bring canned food for a local soup kitchen or a new toy for kids at a local shelter. The feeling you'll get from helping others—from giving—will be better than any present you could ever receive! Learn more about the joys of giving at KidsFixingHearts.org.

CHAPTER TEN

Putting the Cool in School

When we share our knowledge
and good works with others,
we turn the world into our
classroom where we learn
the most important
lessons about life.

The Scholar

by

Chelsea Kirk

O ver the past few years, I have seen many students come and go in my English classroom. In fact, at times it feels as though my classroom is kind of like a Ferris wheel, and at each stop, new students climb on and former students hop off.

I teach at the Maya Angelou Academy in Washington, D.C. I started there as a Teach for America corps member and after my two-year commitment was over, I stayed on to continue teaching English. Maya Angelou Academy is located within the District of Columbia's secure, male juvenile detention center, which is called New Beginnings Youth Development Center. The unique context of my school brings forth the very raw emotions of students as they enter a facility like this, not to mention a new school, and begin to rebuild and transform their identities, their lives and their minds so that they can reenter the community as young men who have more life options.

At age 25, I'm not much older than many of these young men. As a teacher, I have watched our students—whom we call "scholars"—realize their potential within an environment of high expectations and supportive adults. My story is about one of these scholars, and how he holds a very special place in my mind and in my heart.

Like so many others, he entered my classroom as a young man with anger carried on his sleeve. This scholar found himself constantly fighting, trying to conform and adjust to his new surroundings and really trying to figure out who he was as a young man. For the first two months of the school year, his knowledge and wisdom were veiled by his defiance. Then, through both internal and external struggles, a moment appeared in class, a moment in which this scholar started a new chapter of his life.

We were working on a unit where we studied speeches. All of the scholars read countless speeches and studied them for their messages and powerful content. At the end of the unit, each scholar was asked to write his own speech on the topic of power.

With this writing assignment, this particular scholar came to life in the classroom. His anger transformed into participation and he became animated and energized. And his daily class work became high-quality work that showed his true understanding of the material. It became clear that he had reached a turning point, as both a student and a young man. This is the type of turning point that every teacher hopes every student reaches.

For many days, the scholar worked tirelessly on writing and revising his speech. He didn't want any assistance or guidance from me or for anyone to look at his speech until it was finished. When he was done, he entitled his speech, "The Power of Education."

In his speech, he wrote many things, but his focus was on the importance of education. He stressed that young men like him needed a "strong education to get through life," using as his argument that with an education, one could get a good job, have a house and raise a family. He wrote about how helping your family was something everyone should think about when they are young, so when they got older, they wouldn't have to worry about paying all the bills "with a low paying job." His point was that a solid education was the key to a successful life.

When I read his speech, I had one of those moments as a teacher where I said in my head, *He gets it!* This scholar's transformation once again reminded me why I became a teacher in the first place.

To clarify my "He gets it!" comment, I'm not referring to the actual speech—structure- or style-wise—but instead to his new understanding of the cycle of life. I was proud of his transforming his mindset of wanting more from life and also his growing desire to create a life of countless options through a good education. This scholar was able to express himself by writing in a way that urgently stated his beliefs in the power of education and the need for everyone to fundamentally believe in the necessity of education. This young man was proud of his speech, and, yes, proud of the hard work it took to create a final product. I believe he was also proud of his progress and shift in vision.

There are countless scholars who have gotten on and off that Ferris wheel that is my English classroom, feeling broken by the education system and hopeless about education in general. For many of these scholars, education has become something that is no longer a part of their lives or seen as a benefit to their lives.

Yet, if I, as a teacher, can help to transform our scholars' mindsets to re-engage in education and to once more believe that, yes, they need to have an education, then I have succeeded in something so much greater than myself. If I can inspire my students to realize that they are smart and education is not only a necessity in life but a central need to have a life that moves away from crime and toward success, then I have made progress as a teacher and we have triumphed as a school.

The scholar also brought up a topic in his speech I found quite interesting, and, in many cases of the teens I see coming through my classroom, very true; he said that most young people like himself thought only about status symbols when it came to material items "like wearing the best name-brand shoes and clothes." Possessing these high-end items was the most important thing in their lives. He argued that if you had an education, you could have anything you wanted.

The end of the speech was my favorite part, as it came as a complete surprise to me. The scholar wrote that an education was also important so that negative people couldn't "tell you wrong . . . education is power." He exprssed that if you are educated, you'll learn the difference between right and wrong. For these young men, that is a very important lesson.

The power of education can make you realize so many things. And though there's much resistance when these scholars enter my classroom, over time and with much patience on everyone's part, those walls begin to fall. These scholars begin to learn something even greater than what can be found in a textbook, and so do I.

Beneath the anger, frustration, hopelessness and irritation, there is the realization that education—yes, education—can give you power.

Chelsea

KNOWLEDGE IS POWER!

Chelsea is a teacher at Maya Angelou Academy's New Beginnings Youth Development Center and a former Teach for America corps member. The more you learn about different subjects and different interests, the more you will expand your vision and empower yourself to achieve anything you set your mind to! Please visit SeeForever.org (click on Forever Foundation/Maya Angelou Schools) and TeachForAmerica.org.

Because She is a Girl

by

Sarah Musa

Imagine a six-year-old girl sitting on the side of her yard in Afghanistan. She eagerly watches as her younger brothers head off to school. Meanwhile, she fantasizes about the day she will have the opportunity to go to school and proudly wear her school uniform. She has dreams and aspirations about her future, but unfortunately without an education, she will not realize her potential. She feels a sense of animosity growing inside her because she feels oppressed by her society. She knows that she is not permitted to go to school simply because SHE IS A GIRL.

I became aware of the denial of girls' rights to education, especially in developing countries, four years ago. It was around that time that my friend Rachel introduced me to Girls Learn International (GLI). The goal of GLI is to provide girls worldwide with an education. I was touched the most when I heard stories of girls in some developing countries who were sneaking off to the forests with their school supplies in order to continue their learning. That was the turning point for me to offer help to those girls.

In September 2009, with the help of Rachel and some GLI staff members, including Ms. Choudhury, Ms. Salthouse and Ms. Steimer-King, I started a Girls Learn International chapter at my high school in Virginia and we partnered with a group of girls in India. These girls are unable to attend school because of their parents' preference for educating a boy over a girl, as well as economic constraints.

I am filled with passion for girls who are deprived of education because I know that education plays an important role as a foundation for a young persons' development toward adult life. While serving as president of my high school's GLI chapter, I ensured that our chapter established strong communication with our partner school in India. For instance, we wrote the girls letters at the beginning of each school year to see how they were doing and also to learn of their plans. Every year, the responses received from our partner school motivated me to inspire my team members to make more contributions for them.

Through fundraising activities, our team has been able to raise more than $1,700. The fundraising activities we organized over the years included bake sales, selling Indian bracelets and holding movie screenings. Henna tattoos done by Azka, a GLI member, were also a popular fundraising activity. Proceeds from these fundraising activities were transmitted to our partner school through the GLI headquarters. Our efforts increased the number of underprivileged girls in India having access to education, which makes me very proud.

Through our Girls Learn International chapter, I learned that I should never take anything for granted, especially the right to get an education. I believe that with freedom of education, girls can become the brightest and most successful leaders.

Now, as a freshman at James Madison University, I hope to build upon my high school efforts and to continue to be an inspiration and advocate for girls around the world. My mission is stronger than ever: No one should ever be denied an education or equal rights simply because she is a girl.

Sarah

VALUE YOUR EDUCATION!

Sarah is the co-founder of the Girls Learn International chapter at her high school. No matter your circumstances, if you are fortunate enough to attend school, value the education you are getting and make the most of it—take advantage of every opportunity your school offers. Never forget that in some places, as Sarah points out, young people, especially girls, are not able to go to school. Please visit GirlsLearn.org.

From Our Field to Yours

by

Olivia Wong

Several years ago, a San Francisco homeless man taught me a valuable lesson about helping people in need. This was a lesson I would eventually use to help young people halfway around the globe.

Upon returning home from my sophomore year at the University of California, Santa Barbara, I carefully organized a duffel bag of ordinary household items to give to a local homeless man whom I had seen in my neighborhood since I was a child. I compiled items I assumed this homeless man could use: socks, a blanket, medicine, toiletries, books, Ziploc bags, instant coffee, water, nail clippers and a glass coin jar. After finding him on the street, I approached him and initiated a conversation.

When I asked if he could find any of the contents useful, he shook his head "no" and dismissed me without saying one word. Shocked by this unexpected response, I immediately apologized for interrupting his day. Feeling helpless and embarrassed, I carried the heavy duffel bag back home in silence.

Regret consumed my thoughts: *I should have asked him why he did not want my duffel bag of items. Perhaps the offer unintentionally belittled him or maybe he truly had no use for mundane objects like socks and nail clippers.* But lacking the courage to confront his decision, I did not ask. I cannot think of a time I was more disappointed in myself.

Coincidentally, on that same day I heard a story about how REI, a popular outdoor-goods retailer, had donated a generous amount of sophisticated, weather-resistant thermal tents to refugees in Afghanistan. The company was later perplexed, much like I was in my own fruitless attempt, to find that their tents were set ablaze and billowed with smoke. After receiving the tents, the refugees had ignited them because propane fuel was scarce and the refugees were in dire need of heat rather than luxurious, wind-resistant shelters.

After seeing that story, I realized that although my actions were driven by a sincere concern for the welfare of the homeless man, I was not in a position to make an assumption about how best to help him. I have never been homeless nor have I experienced the realities of poverty—the dearth of basic necessities and material possessions. The material items that I attach importance to may hold little value to the homeless man, much like the shelters provided to those Afghanistan refugees.

When my personal experience converged with my new understanding of humanitarian assistance, a meaningful lesson grew in my heart and mind. In order to address a pressing issue, one cannot rely merely on good intentions. By failing to have a clear understanding of an issue and its underlying factors, one can produce more negative effects than good. However, by being conscious of the perspective of the people in need, and working directly with a person or group, one has the potential to overcome unforeseen challenges and effectively alleviate the problem at hand.

Soon after, I learned of a humanitarian crisis that really spoke to my heart. Following the 2010 World Cup, there was a surge of young, innocent children being trafficked because of their aspirations to play soccer. I understood the popularity of soccer from an international perspective. During two years of high school, I lived in a small, remote town in South Eastern Brazil. I recalled how the entire community of Lagoa Santa loved the game of futbol (soccer)—it was common to see children dribbling balls through the red-dust roads or sprinting through narrow streets giving chase to a loose ball, and crowds hunched in front of television sets and exploding with excitement over a goal. Because of their extraordinary passion for the game, I, too, quickly fell in love with the culture of futbol.

Through my research, I discovered that as more and more money started flowing into professional European leagues, the demand for young players grew, specifically in Brazil and West Africa where the demand sky-rocketed. But so did the number of unlicensed agents, illegitimate soccer academies and shady middlemen looking to exploit these players. For a very small percentage of these young players, their dreams of going professional in Europe came true. But the rest faced a litany of horrors—deadly Mediterranean crossings, broken promises, vanishing agents, brutal living conditions and families torn apart.

For children in soccer-crazed nations like Brazil and the Ivory Coast in Africa, a shot at playing professionally is all but irresistible to both children and their parents. This possibility leads parents to value soccer as a path to monetary success, instead of a good education. Thus, families often allocate their life savings for their sons to reach soccer stardom. However, when results do not materialize, players are abandoned, families are conned out of the little life savings they have and soccer scouts move on to new players.

This harsh reality has ignited a vicious cycle of human trafficking, with an estimated 20,000 young African soccer players currently stranded in Europe. In Brazil, cases have become so severe that professional futbol clubs have been banned from the illegal recruitment of minors under the age of 14.

To combat this issue and the actual root of the problem—poverty and the lack of universal primary education—I sought to design an alternative opportunity for children around the world to play soccer while attending school. I founded Inspire a Child with the goal of combating soccer-induced trafficking by building soccer fields and conjoining classrooms as a local solution to increase the quality of education and attendance rates in post-conflict and developing regions of the world. By making classroom attendance compulsory in order to use the field and equipment, we hope to bridge the gap between sport and study and to facilitate the growth of healthy bodies and minds.

Soccer is not only a fun and enjoyable pastime, but a developmental tool that can help improve the lives of children, their families and communities. In countries torn apart by war or extreme poverty, sporting festivities and games can promote good health, teach important values and leadership skills, and even help further girls' education.

As a former athlete myself, I firmly believe that sport is a peace-building exercise where children can learn to become team players, cooperate and have mutual respect for one another. Engaging in teamwork-related activities can also help children overcome social differences. Our goal is to establish partnerships around the world and host World Cup tournaments where the children can experience international travel and play against Inspire a Child teams in different countries.

I often think about that homeless man, and I send him my gratitude for teaching me the importance of truly getting to know and understand our fellow human beings and the causes that we feel most passionate about. That understanding is a first step to changing the world for the better!

Olivia

LEARN FROM THOSE YOU'RE HELPING!

Olivia is the founder of Inspire a Child. One of the biggest lessons Olivia learned is how important it is to really know and understand the people you are trying to help. You can do this by visiting local homeless shelters and speaking with the residents, volunteering at a soup kitchen or helping the residents of a nursing home. There are so many ways to help others! By better understanding those in need, you can more effectively help them. To learn more about Olivia and her work, please visit www.InspireAChildSoccer.com.

Together We are Stronger

by

Ashley Shuyler

My life changed forever at age 11. My parents told me we were going on a family vacation to Tanzania, Africa. I was so excited to see the lions, elephants and giraffes, just like in *The Lion King*. Little did I know that it would be the people I met in Tanzania who would cause me to return to my home in Colorado a changed person.

While in Tanzania, I met kids my same age who were begging on the side of the road. I remember buying a T-shirt from one young boy who couldn't go to school because he had to work to make a living for his family. And I saw students learning in barely-finished classrooms.

But the people I met in Tanzania were the most generous, determined and hard-working people I had ever met, and the friends that I made asked me not to forget them when I returned home to America. That trip made me determined to find a way to support and uplift these people who had such strength and joy.

I returned home to Colorado and, over the next few years, tried to learn about this place that I had visited. I soon discovered that 95 percent of girls in Tanzania don't have the opportunity to complete a high school education, mostly because they can't afford the school fees. The average income in Tanzania is about $2 per day, so when families have to choose to send one of their children to school, they will most often choose to send their son. I had always loved school and my educational opportunities, so I realized that I had found the perfect way to help.

In 2001, when I was 16, I started a nonprofit organization called AfricAid with the mission of supporting girls' education in Tanzania. It took a lot of work and a great deal of support from family and friends. I told everyone I knew about my passion for East Africa and my dream of supporting young women there. Soon, I had a team of friends, local leaders, neighbors and kids assembled who were ready and willing to help. They became our board of directors and helped me raise our first funds. They also sponsored our first 10 scholars, paying for their schooling, and found creative ways to raise awareness for our mission, such as undertaking a fundraising climb of Tanzania's famed Mount Kilimanjaro.

Since that time, we have raised more than $1 million and supported over 40,000 Tanzanian students in their educational goals and with their dreams. We have done that through various programs and projects, including providing scholarships for girls who wouldn't otherwise be able to go to school; building new classrooms at overcrowded schools; purchasing computers and textbooks to increase the quality of education; working with local moms to establish a school lunch program at one rural school; supporting vocational training and teacher training initiatives; and last, starting leadership and entrepreneurship training classes for Tanzanian girls.

For me, the most gratifying aspect of this work has been the opportunity to return to Tanzania each year and hear the incredible stories of the young women we are supporting there. There is one young woman, Theresia, whose story has been a particular source of inspiration for me. In my opinion, her story highlights why I believe that girls' education is so important in places like Tanzania.

Theresia and I are the same age. But Theresia was born in a remote corner of northern Tanzania. And the day after she was born, a man came to Theresia's family and said that he hoped to marry Theresia when she finished primary school (the seventh grade). In exchange for several cattle, Theresia was entered into this arranged marriage.

Her life continued as normal for the next several years, and she started going to primary school. She walked three hours to and from school each day, getting up very early and walking to school in the dark, so that she could sit and study for just a few minutes before school started. Then, she'd return home late in the evenings to do chores, such as gathering firewood and fetching water.

This hard work started to pay off for Theresia, and she soon was at the top of her class. Every time she scored well on her tests, the boys in her class were so upset that a girl was outperforming them that they would taunt her, pinch her and sometimes even throw stones at her. But she didn't give up, and at the end of her seventh grade year, she scored well enough on her national examinations to continue on to secondary school (high school).

As a result, she had to make the difficult decision to postpone her arranged marriage, which was unheard of in her community. In so doing, she became the first girl in her village to go to high school, and AfricAid provided the scholarship for her to go. She is now in teacher-training college, studying to become the first woman teacher in her village. She has also become a true inspiration to the entire generation of girls who will follow her!

Theresia has truly been a source of inspiration for me in my work, and I have gotten to know her through letters exchanged over the years and during lengthy visits with her at her village. For me, her story embodies my favorite Swahili word, one that has a big meaning: *tupo*. In Swahili, tupo means "together we are stronger."

Together, we are so much stronger than we are alone. Together, we can make big changes that will leave this world better than we found it.

And together, we can do so much to uplift the young women around this world who want so much to create a better future for the next generation.

Tupo!

Ashley

THERE IS STRENGTH IN NUMBERS!

Ashley is the founder of AfricAid. Just like Ashley learned, when you join forces with others in your school, your community or halfway around the world, you can accomplish so much more than by working alone. Join Ashley's crusade at AfricAid.com.

FO(u)R Fragile Hearts

by

Charles Maceo

Today brought ambivalence, profound joy and great sadness. I am pursuing an acting career where it can be very easy to focus on myself. But I am also a young teacher, and I find situations and people in my life who help me to not become too self-absorbed. We all must look at ourselves through the eyes of others, to keep us humble and alert.

What seemed to be a fairly benign altercation between four young girls—ages nine and 10—in my inner-city acting class turned out to be far more serious. While visiting the imaginary Shakespearean world of the Capulets and Montagues in *Romeo & Juliet*, I was quickly brought back to reality when the tension and hatred between four elementary age girls far exceeded the intense animosity of the characters in the play we were rehearsing.

I called the young ladies aside to settle their issues. As the girls began to vent their frustrations, I became keenly aware that this was a sort of three-versus-one, racially-motivated situation. Three young Hispanic girls lashed out with insults, stories and frustrations toward one African-American girl. Back and forth, the girls exchanged words and accusations that were all deeply, deeply rooted in pain.

As I listened to them, I made it abundantly clear that I would not participate in their animosity or spend time figuring out "who did what to whom" so that some sort of "punishment" could be given to "teach a lesson." I was solely interested in where their pain stemmed from.

I told the girls, "Hurt people like to hurt people. We often tend to be afraid and ignore what really, truly bothers us on the inside, and frustration and anger are manifested into hateful actions and words that we often regret, yet cannot seem to control."

Soon after, the girls began to open up to me.

One young girl had tears flowing down her cheeks as she admitted the anger she held was a result of her deceased mother and a father addicted to drugs. No longer hidden was the pain of not having either parent in her life, and being raised by extended family members.

Another girl had admirable candor, yet it was incredibly painful to hear as she told me about the anger she held inside because she had been raped, as well as the gang violence that surrounded her at home. She also had parents who seemed more interested in consuming drugs than being present in her life.

The third girl announced how she knew her anger came from the absence of a father whom she felt didn't love her and whom she had not seen since she was one. She and the others felt that their respective and collective worlds instructed them to react in ways they ignorantly deemed as best, with fists aimed to inflict pain and words that endeavored to scar the very hearts and lives of others.

The last student sat silently with eyes that purposefully rolled, but yet always seemed on the brink of tears. Her attitude aspired to nonchalance, but screamed insecurity. Her words were very few, but the silence that sprung forth was filled with agony. Alarmingly, even in the midst of tears, the girls still continued the insults.

As if divinely ordered, the principal walked in and saw the faces of these young girls. With grace and love, the principal quickly broke those self-imposed walls of confusion with words and hugs that penetrated and uplifted the girls' spirits.

Across the room, I then sat with two of the girls, one at a time. As my hands held their faces, their eyes released tears of pain as I told each of them, "None of this is your fault. All the bad things that have happened to you—parents, rape, gangs, the anger—it's not your fault."

I then asked the two of them, "You don't like feeling this way, do you?"

Without hesitation, they shook their heads "no."

I continued, "All I care about is each of you becoming a better person. You're so sweet. So beautiful. So smart. I don't want your anger to get the best of you and continue to make you say and do things you never wanted to."

I further told them, "I'm here to fight this with you. It'll take practice and sometimes, you'll make a mistake. But as long as you keep trying to better yourself, that's what counts."

Frowned faces turned into half-smiles that suggested unlimited hope in what may come. It's moments like these that bring me to the state of ambivalence I initially mentioned: joy that I, as a teacher, have identified a problem that I can somehow assist in finding solutions to, yet sadness that the problem itself ever existed in the first place, especially in the world of children.

It's moments like these that remind me why I work with children and specifically the nonprofit City Hearts: Kids Say "Yes" to the Arts in Los Angeles. Through this avenue and wonderful organization, I have been given joy, power, ability and insight to help children on a daily basis.

It's moments like these that remind me of the mission of City Hearts, which is to not only provide access to the arts, but to provide it at the highest of standards. Also, to give at-risk students in some of the most economically distressed neighborhoods of Southern California experiences that cultivate artistic ability, self-esteem, social and academic skills and creativity, all while strengthening the health and vitality of our community.

It's moments like these that remind me that ultimately we are striving to enable OUR children and youth to be confident, imaginative, tolerant, generous and contributing members of our society.

And finally, it's moments like these that remind me why I am overjoyed to work with children who are often forgotten and ignored by society. As a teacher, I am here to protect their innocence, help graduate them from their states of ignorance to enlightenment and, most of all, to give them the tangible and unequivocal love they deserve in order to grow and become forgiving, benevolent, joyous and healed people. Then, in turn, they will seek to do the same toward others who were once like them.

Charles

SAY "YES" TO A HAPPIER YOU!

Charles is a teacher at City Hearts: Kids Say "Yes" to the Arts. Don't be afraid to ask someone—a teacher, a parent, a friend—for help with your problems or other challenges in your life, no matter how big or small they may be. Remember: You deserve to be happy! To check out a really happy and fun place, please visit CityHearts.org.

The World Lies in the Hands of a Girl

by

<u>Sophia and Nadia Tareen</u>

Protected behind the tinted windows of our large van, we examined the Pakistani city at a distance as we overtook most of the smaller cars on the bustling streets. The relentless ruckus of the Karachi traffic faded into the background as we trekked into rural Sindh. With our suitcase stocked with notebooks and gifts, we readied ourselves for the visit to the school we had only envisioned in our minds.

We are two sisters from Philadelphia who are working to spark positive global progress in this often-mystifying world. Going to an all-girls school, feminism and gender equality have been ingrained into our attitudes and views. Whenever we hear news headlines about gender discrimination, we simultaneously look at each other with a grimace, acknowledging the mutual feeling of disgust. Throughout the world, girls are denied access to an education, a fundamental right established in the Universal Declaration of Human Rights by the United Nations. Girls are deprived of this right to an education for reasons such as financial barriers, safety concerns and cultural preferences for boys.

Currently, two-thirds of the 121 million uneducated children in the world are girls. Without an education, these girls fall into the perpetual cycle of poverty, which exposes them to extreme forms of violence, sexual exploitation and more forms of abuse. While these facts are indeed staggering, we can assure you that these numbers are real and these stories are real. We know this because we have had not one, but two extraordinary opportunities to meet the brave girls who defy the limitations of their circumstances and make it a priority to receive an education.

In 2007, we learned about Girls Learn International (GLI), a Los Angeles-based organization dedicated to empowering and encouraging students in the U.S. to help their counterparts in the developing world go to school. We started our own GLI chapter at our all-girls school, the Baldwin School in Bryn Mawr, Pennsylvania and established a partnership with the Khanott girls' school in the rural Sindh region of Pakistan, the country where our parents grew up.

We spent the early years of the Baldwin GLI chapter developing a strong foundation for the club through expanding membership and conducting interactive meetings, holding stimulating assemblies and unique events. During the year, we introduced and discussed human rights issues with the student members and fostered cross-cultural communication between the Baldwin and Khanott students through individualized pen pal letters. By the end of the first year, our chapter had grown to 30 dedicated members, and our motivation to promote universal education had been bolstered.

In 2008, our parents presented the two of us with a remarkable opportunity—a trip to Pakistan to visit the Khanott School. The Baldwin GLI chapter prepared by drafting letters and creating beaded friendship bracelets for the Pakistani students. As we bid our Baldwin classmates farewell before winter break, we both felt the immense responsibility bestowed upon us. To represent both the Baldwin School and GLI was an overwhelming honor. However, rather than apprehension, we were driven by the prospect of making an impact on the Pakistani students, our American classmates and our own outlooks.

We arrived in Karachi and were greeted by our family who lived there. A few days after we settled in, we packed the gifts from the Baldwin students and made our way to rural Sindh.

We made a sharp turn off the highway into the sandy terrain and pulled into the Khanott village. A representative from the Indus Resource Center—an organization that sets up schools for social and economic development in Pakistan—led us into the Khanott School where we were enthusiastically greeted with *Assalamu alaikum*—may peace be upon you.

The students were ecstatic about our presence and their eagerness to learn about our lives in America was clear.

First, we presented the fourth grade class with the Baldwin GLI chapter's cultural exchange project: a scrapbook containing photos of our chapter's members, the Baldwin School and wintertime in Pennsylvania. We also distributed the friendship bracelets and introductory letters that our chapter had written and our mother had translated into Urdu, the language of Pakistan. We then visited the sixth-grade classroom where the girls told us that they hoped to continue their education at a university.

We showed the Pakistani students where the Baldwin School and the Khanott village were located on a map of the world. Even though the girls of Baldwin and the girls of Khanott are geographically thousands of miles apart from each other, we are all students, striving to gain more knowledge about the world we live in, trying to shape our futures and discover our paths in life.

This trip's poignancy transformed both of our understandings of the dire situation of girls' rights—it made the mission real. Upon returning home, we organized musical evenings, fashion shows, guest speakers and assemblies in which we discussed the Khanott girls' stories and fundraised more than $3,000 for our partner school. Our GLI chapter also worked with the entire upper school at Baldwin to make and send the Khanott School a colorful quilt, with each square featuring a word representing our values and beliefs in both English and Urdu. For example, "freedom" is *azadi*, "hope" is *umeed* and "believe" is *yakeen*.

Three years later, we contacted the Khanott School directors again and coordinated another visit into rural Sindh. This time, we were prepared and resolutely conveyed our mission to the Baldwin School administration. More than 100 upper school students wrote personal letters inside the front covers of hand-decorated notebooks for the Khanott School students. We wanted to express how much we valued our friendship with the students and our appreciation for the beautiful bangles, handmade traditional dolls and other local handicrafts they had sent us. We gathered notebooks and an assortment of other American gifts into a suitcase, and once more the two of us made the daylong journey from Philadelphia to Karachi.

After a beautiful drive through the dusty, rural landscape of Sindh to the Khanott village, the students of our partner school greeted us at the door with that same inspiring charisma as they had during our first visit. Joy and pride ran through us as we walked by Baldwin's colorful quilt, which was displayed outside one of the classrooms. Through construction efforts, the school had expanded in size, the classrooms were better organized and the students were as eager to learn as before.

The girls described their daily routine to us and explained how attending school has allowed them to avoid the fate of many of their mothers—child marriage. One 15-year-old girl named Benazeer described how she had brought her school lessons into her home by teaching her younger sisters about the importance of receiving an education. Sitting next to her, another student named Sidra explained how she planned on becoming a teacher at the Khanott School once she graduated. A girl named Saira told us about how she was arranged to marry an older man when she was only 15, but the Khanott School teachers rallied behind her and convinced her family to allow her to continue her education and get married when she was ready.

As we listened, we felt the power of the girls' courageous stories. Through their commanding voices, we heard their determination to become educated. And through their resolution to break the barriers before them, we saw the value of the investment. Keeping girls in school is a real solution to the epidemic of poverty that affects the political, economic and social systems of Pakistan.

Girls like Saira are the ones who spark change by participating in household and community decisions, standing up for women's basic rights, and protecting other girls from falling into the traps of outdated and discriminatory customs. Girls like Benazeer will end the vicious intergenerational cycles of inequality and poverty. And brave girls like legendary Pakistani activist Malala Yousafzai, who at age 15 was shot by the Taliban and nearly died for her beliefs that every girl deserves an education, are the role models for courageous protestors of injustice. These inspiring young women are the ones who will instill real and purposeful change in communities that would otherwise stagnate in archaic conventions. Girls are the solution that can move the world forward.

We are two sisters asking all of you who are fortunate to live in countries where education is widely accessible to stand up and take action! Global progress starts with giving a girl a chance, a chance made possible if she is put into a school. Join us and we can change the world.

Nadia (second from left) and Sophia (far right)

BECOME PART OF SOMETHING BIGGER THAN YOURSELF!

Sophia and Nadia are co-founders of the Girls Learn International chapter at their school. Join these sisters in helping girls attend school in places like Pakistan, and in the process you will become an important part of a global movement! To start your own Girls Learn International chapter, please visit GirlsLearn.org.

CHAPTER ELEVEN

Live Out LOUD!

Through our words and actions,
each one of us can give
a voice and inspiration
to the voiceless,
creating a loud
and positive
impact on
the world.

Speak Up
and Step Out!

by

Delaitre Hollinger

My love for the community in which I live in Florida, and those who live in it, began when I was a fourth grader at Hartsfield Elementary School. The rat in my science class had given birth to babies and my science teacher was going to feed them to the class snake. I said, "No you're not!" I then started a school-wide campaign and petition to save the baby rats. It worked and I took two of them home with me.

I realized then that I wanted to help others. Even as a fourth-grade student, and virtually powerless, I knew that in the future when I saw something that I felt was wrong or unjust, I would do whatever I could to right that wrong.

My mother, Delois, was adamant about getting me involved in local sports and organizations when I was a child. Her love and caring commitment to my well-being has always been her priority. I cherish her for that. The organization with which she got me involved that would have the most lasting impact was Big Brothers Big Sisters of the Big Bend.

When my first Big Brother had to leave me after two years, I was very reluctant to get another one. But the agency then matched me with Brent Hartsfield, an engineer, and we've been together ever since. Brent instilled courage and independence in me. Whenever I told him that I felt like doing something, he would say, "Go for it!"

Brent also encouraged me to excel in the academic area of math, which was never my favorite subject. Being active within the local community, he has always attended the many events, recitals and awards banquets I have been privileged to be a part of, and I will always be grateful to him for that.

Brent and I were so excited to learn that he was nominated for and won the local, state and national Big Brother of the Year award for 2012. We traveled to Washington, D.C. to meet President Obama, and it was an experience I will never forget.

I have always been somewhat of a historian, which contributed to my involvement in community relations. This also started with my mother. She would not read traditional bedtime stories to me. Instead, she would read stories of great Americans like Martin Luther King, Jr., Mary McLeod Bethune and John F. Kennedy. She told me how they all grew up to change the world around them.

"You can be anything you want to be," my mother always told me.

That made me really think, *What around me can I change?* A huge opportunity presented itself when I turned 18 years old. I filed to run for a seat on the city commission.

I was active in my community prior to running for office. My neighborhood is in Southern Tallahassee, which historically has always been neglected. My first presentation before the county commission was to name a park for two great leaders in my community. Met with little resistance, the measure passed unanimously! That was my first big community project and accomplishment.

After that, I began to speak out against the closing of the Gwen Cherry Child Development Center. I spoke in favor of funding for the Leon County Mental Health Court. And I advocated for Gibbs Cottage, the oldest building at Florida A&M University. Constructed in 1894, the abandoned home was in need of repairs. As of this writing, the cottage is going through an extensive renovation process.

People began to listen to me when I spoke. I realized that even a teenager can bring about positive change in his or her community.

As a candidate for office, I brought to light that my community needed a new voice in local government. Having just graduated from high school, I ran on my record of community service, rather than on my educational background and qualifications. I was one candidate in a six-man race. Among those running for the seat were a former Tallahassee mayor and other men who were decades older than I was. In the end, nearly 1,200 Tallahassee residents voted for me, demonstrating their trust in me to serve them on the city commission.

However, I did not win the election. But I was still victorious in my pursuit for many of the issues that I championed, such as a city website with easily accessible records for residents and turning abandoned buildings into venues for homeless residents. I also suggested that vacant lots where people loitered could be used for community gardens. All of these things have now been implemented in the city of Tallahassee and Leon County.

At Tallahassee Community College, I serve my school community as a student senator, Constitutional Review Committee chair and intercollegiate ambassador to Florida A&M University with the Student Government Association. I was also selected to attend the National Student Leadership, Citizenship and Advocacy Conference because of my leadership in the student senate. I have been a senator since being elected by my colleagues in September 2012.

When I arrived on campus a week after the primary election on August 14, I found many things that needed to be done. When I was officially appointed, I introduced bills for decreasing on-campus smoking, establishing building designations and creating a pedestrian safety program and an intercampus shuttle system, among other things. I was selected for the position because of what I had already been able to accomplish by simply making my voice heard in Tallahassee.

I grew up in a single-parent household. It not only helps to have a good mother who cares about your well-being, but you have to be the one who is willing to make a change. Unfortunately, there most likely will always be injustices around all of us. If you feel that something is not right, it is your duty and God-given purpose to speak up, step out and do something about it!

Delaitre

INSPIRE CHANGE!

Delaitre is the "Little Brother" to the 2012 Big Brothers Big Sisters of America "Big Brother of the Year." Delaitre's many activities demonstrate how he saw the need for changes in his community and he stepped up by volunteering and running for office to help make those changes become a reality. You, too, can inspire change and progress at your school by running for student council or volunteering to help make your school and community a happier, healthier place for everyone. Please visit BBBS.org and BigBendMentoring. org (Big Brothers Big Sisters of the Big Bend).

Stopping Hate in Its Tracks

by

Emily-Anne Rigal

I was bullied. At the time, I felt like I was the only one, but the truth is that two out of three teens endure verbal or physical harassment every year and each one has his or her own story. This is mine.

In elementary school, my classmates tormented me for being overweight. Each morning, I crossed my fingers in hopes that it would not be a day when the teacher would let us pick our own partners because I rarely had someone to pair up with. Not having a partner was mortifying, but even worse was the daily loneliness I endured. It got so bad that I eventually switched schools.

Throughout middle and high school, my self-confidence gradually increased. The more I accepted myself, the less disconnected I felt from my peers and the happier I became.

Overcoming my personal struggle with bullying and loneliness inspired me to create WeStopHate when I was 16 years old. WeStopHate is a nonprofit program changing the way we teens view ourselves by collectively helping each of us to accept, embrace and love who we are.

I now know the benefits of accepting myself for who I am. But memories are made to last, and even the painful ones have a purpose. So my heart goes out to those struggling with self-acceptance. I believe it is my life's work to help others turn self-hatred into self-love.

When creating WeStopHate, I knew others could relate to what I had gone through, so I chose to lead by example and make videos sharing my personal stories. I subjected myself to ridicule by exposing my innermost thoughts and feelings because I believe honesty is the most effective way to generate a sincere response. It was as if there was a piece of me in each viewer, and instead of criticizing me, teen viewers respected my authenticity.

Still, I believed growing WeStopHate depended on the power of teens coming together and that direct teen involvement was essential for the program to thrive. For this reason, I organized a team of teen volunteers across the country to begin spreading the WeStopHate message.

WeStopHate is more than just an anti-bullying program. It's a call to action to stop hate: stop hating yourself, stop hating others, stop letting others hate you. WeStopHate reminds teens that stopping hate isn't something to do once, but it's a practice and approach to live by each day.

Our reason for focusing on teen-esteem is simple: only when we see a rise in self-esteem will we see a decline in bullying. This is because people who are happy with themselves won't put others down. Stopping bullying means putting an end to the lifelong, painful consequences each victim suffers, and that creates a better world for us all.

What makes WeStopHate special is that we address bullying in a teen-centered way. We know peer pressure is typically a source for negativity, but seeing that teens have the power to help other teens leads us to believe that peer pressure can also be a source for good.

Furthermore, we understand how to use the power of digital media for good by allowing it to shape the way we see ourselves and how others see us, consequently preempting bullies.

We are not yet close to ending all forms of bullying. But in just a few years' time, WeStopHate has made a difference in the lives of tens of thousands of teens, and we are eager to make an even greater impact moving forward. Our goal is to continue creating a platform that will give each teen across the globe who dreams of a world without the pain of bullying the opportunity to do something about stopping the hate and living the life they deserve.

Emily-Anne

ACCEPT WHO YOU ARE!

Emily-Anne is the founder of WeStopHate. Stopping hate begins with you! You have so many gifts and talents to share with the world—you have a purpose for being here. Discover what those gifts are and learn to love what is unique about yourself. Also learn to love and accept what is unique about the people around you, and turn peer pressure into a force for good. Take the first step by checking out WeStopHate.org and EmilyAnneRigal.com.

A Life Worth Living

by

Frank Stephens

I am a young man with Down syndrome and my life is worth living. I want to tell you a story about the power of choosing positive over negative, respect over meanness and kindness over anger. It is also very much a story of how the power of the Internet can magnify a mission you believe is beyond your wildest dreams.

But, before I tell my story, I need to tell you a little about what it means to have Down syndrome and why I need to state that my life is worth living. There are a lot of misunderstandings about people like me—people with Down syndrome and others who have intellectual disabilities. Many people act as if we don't have the same feelings, desires and goals as the rest of you. I want you to know that isn't true.

We are a little different from the rest of you. For instance, I like to point out that people with Down syndrome are about two percent greater than the rest of you. That's because we have one more chromosome in every cell of our bodies than you do. That extra chromosome does create differences. Sometimes, that one chromosome makes us look a little different around the eyes and nose. Other times, it gives us shorter arms and legs. Those aren't very important, but some of the other differences are that we never develop certain kinds of cancer, and scientists studying our chromosomes may someday develop a cure for cancer. Also, we have some material in our brains that is similar to the brains of older people who have Alzheimer's disease. We may prove helpful to finding a cure for that, too.

As most of you know, the most noticeable difference that people with an intellectual disability have is that we process information more slowly, and sometimes less clearly than the rest of you. That is what led to us being described, in science, as people with "mental retardation." That just means our mental process is slowed down compared with other people. Unfortunately, some unkind people created a slang word from that scientific description that was used first to insult people like me directly and later to try to insult others by comparing them to people like me.

That insulting slang word is "retard."

I have mostly been lucky in my life. I grew up in a family that encouraged me to believe I could grow up and make a difference in the world. My little brother, who is two years younger, was ready to challenge anyone who tried to pick on me. However, he could not always be at my side. Other kids did sometimes call me names, like "retard," and it hurt. More often, others just assumed I did not have anything to add to their conversations and simply ignored me. That hurt, too.

You see, we do have the same feelings as the rest of you. It hurts to be called a name that is intended to describe me as slow, dumb or shallow. It hurts to be treated as if I am not there.

I made the decision early in my life to just keep coming back and keep engaging in conversations with anyone who would listen. I decided to get into drama classes and act out the characters I wanted to be in real life. When I thought I needed help to further improve myself, I was not afraid to ask for it.

Over time, that led to my speaking on behalf of others with intellectual disabilities. I discovered that I could make people laugh, and, at the same time, make them think about what it was like to have an intellectual disability. I was proud to become a voice for others like me who find it hard to speak for themselves.

My public speaking earned me a place as a Sargent Shriver Global Messenger for Special Olympics and gave me hundreds of opportunities to reach out to people and deliver our organization's message of respect. In Special Olympics, we focus on people's abilities and we respect them for whatever they bring to the rest of us. That is how "respect" has become our favorite R-word. Through our "Spread the Word to End the Word" campaign, we have been working very hard to try to get people—especially young people—to stop using the other R-word as an insult. This brings me back to the story I wanted to tell you.

In 2012, on the evening of the last presidential debate between Mitt Romney and President Barack Obama, a very famous political commentator tweeted that she was glad Mr. Romney had been "kind and gentle to the retard," referring to President Obama. The next morning, Tim Shriver, the chairman and CEO of Special Olympics, asked if I would write a response to the political commentator. I said I would, but I was so angry at first that it was hard to start.

I felt that maybe I should just give up. If an educated person like this commentator could use the R-word to insult the President of the United States, maybe there was just no hope of convincing people how hurtful that word was to people like me. But part of me knew that not everyone feels like she does.

As I began to write, I realized that I needed to stay positive and invite the commentator to become a better person. I worked all day, with some help on spelling and organization from my younger brother and my dad. I finally finished the letter at six o'clock that night. My dad told me that it was so late in the day that probably only a few people would read the letter when Special Olympics posted it on their website. Boy, was he wrong! Within 24 hours, more than 2.5 million people had read my letter. In less than one month, nearly four million people had read it. The next two weeks were crazy. I gave interviews to newspapers, radio shows and TV networks from all over the world.

The responses to my letter were overwhelmingly positive. It was a reminder that we have no idea how powerful we can be when we assume the best about others and just decide to embrace doing the right thing.

Here is the letter I wrote:

Dear [commentator's name],

Come on [commentator's name], you aren't dumb and you aren't shallow. So why are you continually using a word like the R-word as an insult? I'm a 30-year-old man with Down syndrome who has struggled with the public's perception that an intellectual disability means that I am dumb and shallow. I am not either of those things, but I do process information more slowly than the rest of you.

In fact, it has taken me all day to figure out how to respond to your use of the R-word last night. I thought first of asking whether you meant to describe the President as someone who was bullied as a child by people like you, but rose above it to find a way to succeed in life as many of my fellow Special Olympians have.

Then I wondered if you meant to describe him as someone who has to struggle to be thoughtful about everything he says, as everyone else races from one snarky sound bite to the next. Finally, I wondered if you meant to degrade him as someone who is likely to receive bad health care, live in low-grade housing with very little income and still manages to see life as a wonderful gift. Because, [commentator's name], that is who we are—and much, much more.

After I saw your Tweet, I realized you just wanted to belittle the President by linking him to people like me. You assumed that people would understand and accept that being linked to someone like me is an insult and you assumed you could get away with it and still appear on TV. I have to wonder if you considered other hateful words but recoiled from the backlash.

Well, you, and society, need to learn that being compared to people like me should be considered a badge of honor. No one overcomes more than we do and still loves life so much. Come join us someday at Special Olympics. See if you can walk away with your heart unchanged.

A friend you haven't made yet,

John Franklin Stephens
Global Messenger
Special Olympics Virginia

Frank

ASSUME THE BEST ABOUT OTHERS!

Frank is a Sargent Shriver Global Messenger for Special Olympics and an advocate for the Spread the Word to End the Word Campaign. One of the many lessons to be learned from Frank's story is when you expect the best from others, you are often rewarded by receiving just that. By assuming the best about others, Frank's mission to eliminate the R-word and better educate people about Down syndrome and other disabilities has reached millions. You can join Frank's mission by visiting SpecialOlympics.org and R-word.org (R-word: Spread the Word to End the Word).

Another World
is Possible

by

Joseph Therrien

E ven though I had been very interested in politics for a long time, and
even though I had spent years studying and practicing puppetry, starting when I was around 15 and in high school, I had never figured out a way
to authentically merge my political voice with my theatrical voice. Then I
visited Zuccotti Park in New York City during the height of the Occupy
Wall Street protests, and I was pushed into a new world of artistic activism.

As the colorful and creative community of activists grew at Zuccotti
Park, different groups formed, all trying to use their skills and talents to
help create a more economically and socially just world. I met daily with
other artists to brainstorm ideas and support each other's projects. Eventually, a group of us formed The People's Puppets of Occupy Wall Street. We
started creating giant puppet versions of New York City landmarks, such
as the Statue of Liberty, the Brooklyn Bridge and the Wall Street Bull, as if
the city itself was rising up to join our protests.

We also experimented with satirical puppet shows like *Jack and the
Corporate Beanstalk* to challenge conventional power structures and to
move our audiences closer to challenging those structures themselves. We
were met with different—mostly positive—reactions, but we were never
ignored. As it turned out, puppets are great ambassadors for a revolution.

One of our favorite shows was created from a popular chant at the

Occupy Wall Street events: "We are unstoppable. Another world is possible." That refrain became a rallying cry for our movement as we tried to convince people that there was a better way to live, and that if we worked together we would succeed in manifesting it.

But many outsiders remained skeptical. Another world? What would it look like? How could we change a system that seems so entrenched and incapable of change? People had trouble imagining this new world. And that's where puppets could help!

We realized that we had the power to visually demonstrate what a new reality could look like. So we created large, theater-style building fronts that we would want to see in our city, and we called the setting "Neighborhood Heights." These included The Possible Hospital where healthcare is a guaranteed right and not dependent on your economic status, The University of Opportunity where education is free for all, and The First Local Bank of Honesty, which provides banking as a service to the community, not as an opportunity to use your money to gamble on Wall Street.

We wanted to reach as many people as possible, especially those who wouldn't normally go to the theater. So we decided to take our show onto subway cars and perform for free between stops. In our show, one of us plays the mayor, who gives the occupants of our subway car a quick tour around our new city. During the tour, puppet citizens pop up to talk about what it's like to live there. We play instruments and sing, and after sharing what our vision for the city looks like, we invite the audience to share what they'd like to see in this new city.

We were nervous for the first few performances. New Yorkers have a reputation of being tough, and we didn't know how we would be received, especially in an enclosed performance space where we couldn't leave until the next stop! Would we come off as too heavy-handed? Too cheesy? Not New York-hip enough?

We were pleasantly surprised, however, that our audiences were overwhelmingly supportive of our show and its message. Most performances ended in enthusiastic applause and many sparked a public conversation about what could be possible if we all worked together rather than in competition with each other.

Since we created this show, we now have tested it and tweaked it for different environments. In addition to subway cars, we also perform it on the street, in parks and anywhere else where there are people. We continually update the script to reflect the ever-changing world around us.

We've created workshops with community groups where participants see the show and then build and perform their own dream cities. We also team up with activist organizers who are running campaigns in the communities where we are performing. After the performance, we introduce these representatives and invite interested audience members to have deeper conversations with them. Often this leads to them signing up and becoming part of these campaigns.

I am continually amazed at the power that puppetry has to educate, challenge and inspire those around us. I am convinced that we have only scratched the surface of the transformative power of this art form. As puppeteers, we have an incredible opportunity to help people imagine new worlds. With the rising tide of popular protest in the United States, the time is ripe for interested puppeteers to get out on the streets (and into schools, parks and libraries) and experiment!

It's simple: Find others who are interested, compare notes and collaborate. Your revolution is waiting!

Together, we are unstoppable: Another world is possible.

Joseph with Alma (left) and Morgan (right)

BE UNSTOPPABLE!

Joseph is the co-founder of The People's Puppets of Occupy Wall Street. From an early age, Joseph was interested in puppets and making a positive impact—two interests that he is putting to use in a big way today. His story shows how the interests and skills you have right now can empower you to be unstoppable in pursuing your career and good works in the future. Please visit Facebook.com/OWSPuppetGuild.

I Challenge You

by

Kate Dildy

C all me idealistic, but I imagine a world where we are working in unison toward social justice, with one movement for human rights, dignity and a sustainable future.

I have always been that girl whose birthday wish was for everyone to just get along and stop fighting. I also wished for world peace. As I grew up a bit, I understood that world peace does not happen in the blink of an eye. It happens when people work together. It happens at the local level and it begins with a group of really committed, passionate people who want to change the world.

By starting a small, student-founded and student-run organization that taps into the inspiring world of students' expansive imaginations, we can educate, engage and empower the people around us, while making our communities better places to live. I did this as a junior at Georgetown Day School when I started Young Advocates for Change, a group to hand the reigns of democracy to high school students.

Young people are always questioning the system, trying to stand up to authority and defying the status quo. Usually, adults think these qualities are hurdles to success, but I think they are our greatest tools to rethinking the world. The creativity of youth is our biggest untapped resource. If we direct our energy toward helping other people and apply our creativity to solving our thorny social, political and other issues, we will be one step closer to creating a better world.

Maybe nobody thinks world peace is possible, but I do. Nobody thought that we could go to the moon, but we did. Nobody thought that we could fly huge metal containers full of people in the air, but today we call them airplanes. Nothing is impossible and that is why I believe it is absurd that we have to wait until we are adults to champion great causes or voice our opinions about how our country is run.

We should not have to wait until we are adults to help the world. The world needs help now. The world needs our ideas now. We must remember that the right to vote is not our only voice.

I was in the middle of a program called LearnServe, which empowers high school students like me to be social entrepreneurs. At LearnServe, we were asked to look at a problem in the world and solve it, easy as that! (Well not quite!) One day, the head of the LearnServe program asked a simple question: "What pisses you off?"

This was exactly what I needed. I looked around, and instead of being saddened by what seemed like a crushing world of poverty, hunger and disunity, I felt empowered to come up with a tool to help fix it and to unite people with the same goals. It was then that I came up with the idea for Young Advocates for Change.

It felt good to meet people who cared about the world like I did and it felt good to fit in. Finding the right environment and surrounding yourself with the right people can change how you look at the problems around you. Instead of insurmountable mountains to climb, problems become those fun little hills we used to roll down when we were kids. Remember that? It is actually kind of exciting! And I would say, if you cannot find the right environment, make your own. Carve out your own unique path.

This is the time to take action, when we have the chance, especially before we become adults and we have jobs, bills, kids and who knows what else. This is when we have the time, the energy and the freedom to take chances and explore the world. I wanted other people to feel empowered, too. Luckily, we have the answers to the world's problems at our fingertips. If you and I collaborate with other passionate, caring and ambitious young people to advocate for issues we care about, we can unlock our tremendous imaginations.

We must be the change we want to see in the world. We must be the movement, and however small, it will make a difference.

There is an African proverb that says, "If you think you're too small to make a difference, you haven't spent a night with a mosquito."

So I challenge you to make a difference:

★ I challenge you not just to cast your vote, but to pay attention to the real policies, because that is what really matters. It's not important when a politician with a pretty face says what we want to hear. It's what she or he does in office that matters. We want to hold our government accountable to a higher standard of justice, so that we are constantly vigilant in maintaining our freedom. This is the cure to the corruption that people always complain about in government. We are the cure.

★ I challenge you to start an organization to help your friends learn how to become advocates, to help them organize campaigns and create change so that you can take action for the rest of your life, community by community, city by city, state by state, cause by cause. Start an activism group.

★ I challenge you to spread your ideas. Start thinking globally and acting locally. Most importantly, though, build partnerships and collaborate with each other.

And, finally, I challenge you to believe that YOU are the change the world needs!

Kate

THE WORLD NEEDS YOU RIGHT NOW!

Kate is the founder of Young Advocates for Change at her school. Her message is clear: YOU are what the world needs right now. The world needs you to use your talents, interests and opportunities—to use your voice and your skills—to stand up for what you believe in and lead the way toward a better present and future for the planet and all living beings. Please visit GDS.org (Georgetown Day School) and Learn-Serve.org.

NOW IT'S YOUR TURN TO STAND UP!

It's time to get started on your own mission to help make a difference in the world. In the blank spaces that follow, first write a talent, an interest and a skill you have. Everyone has them, including you! You can start by asking yourself, *What am I really good at doing? What do I like doing?* The answers can be about anything, such as excelling in a certain school subject or sport, playing a musical instrument, partaking in a favorite hobby, hanging out with friends, building things, drawing, painting, cooking, traveling or even having a special place in your heart for animals.

Second, under each answer, brainstorm how you can use that talent, interest and skill to help others, or even the planet, right now at your school, in your community or around the world. Ask yourself questions like, *Is there a need in my school or community that I can help with right now?* Or maybe, *If I could do anything in the world to help the planet or those in need, what would it be?* Let your imagination run wild with the possibilities.

Third, seal the deal by signing The Stand Up! Promise Pledge and gluing or drawing a fun picture of yourself at the end in the space provided. And, finally, join the team of young activists in this book by using your list as a starting point for turning your ideas into a reality!

1. Your Talent: _____
How can you use this talent to help others, or our world, right now?

_____
_____
_____
_____

2. Your Interest: _____
How can you use this interest to help others, or our world, right now?

_____
_____
_____
_____
_____

256

3.Your Skill: _____
How can you use this skill to help others or our world, right now?

_____

_____

_____

_____

The STAND UP! Promise Pledge

I promise to ROCK THE WORLD by using my talents, interests and skills to make my dreams come true and to make a positive difference in my school, community and the world by standing up for our planet and those who are in need!

Sign your name here: _____

Paste your
picture here!

I PROMISE TO STAND UP
FOR A BETTER WORLD!

Acknowledgments

From the moment I started working on *Stand Up!*, I knew it would be one of the most important books I would create in my lifetime. In addition to the young activists, this book is the result of more people than I could ever properly name or adequately thank. These individuals include the parents, guardians and siblings, as well as the organizations, staffs, schools, teachers, volunteers and teams, who support the work being done around the world by these extraordinary story contributors. To each one of you who has helped us move this project forward in ways great and small, please accept every word and every minute of writing and editing that went into creating this book as expressions of my sincerest gratitude. Our work—and the words in this book—would not be possible without your tireless help and support.

The story contributors and I extend a BIG THANKS to Publishing Syndicate. Kudos to Pat Nelson who assisted with copyediting and Alison Carmichael, who illustrated the book's cover. And we must thank our publishers Dahlynn and Ken McKowen; they both supported and understood the groundbreaking nature of this project from the very beginning.

We give a BIG SHOUT OUT to my agent, Steve Troha at Folio Literary Management, who did what he does best and pulled this project together. Just as my contributors in this book are blazing new pathways with their good works, Steve is forging new and compassionate pathways within the literary world.

And, finally, to the story contributors—those luminous co-authors with whom I share these pages—you are my superheroes, and I am your biggest fan! Thank you for inviting me to share in your amazing journeys.

LONG MAY YOU ROCK THE WORLD! +++++

~~ John Schlimm

About John Schlimm

John Schlimm is an activist, artist, educator and the international award-winning author of several books on cooking and entertaining, history, how-to and fiction.

His ongoing community-based efforts include serving more than 20 years as an activist and advocate for healthy living, education and the arts through his work with such organizations as Citizens Against Physical, Sexual & Emotional Abuse, the American Cancer Society, the American Red Cross and The Humane Society.

He has traveled the country making appearances and speaking about inspirational and motivational topics, cooking and entertaining, and public relations to a wide variety of groups, including his commencement address at the University of Pittsburgh at Bradford where he has taught in the communication and the arts department.

John, who holds a master's degree in education from Harvard University, has appeared on *The Ellen DeGeneres Show*, *Martha Stewart Living's Everyday Food*, NPR's *The Splendid Table*, *QVC* and *Fox & Friends* and has been featured in *The New York Times*.

Connect with John
Facebook: www.Facebook.com/JohnSchlimm
Twitter: @JohnSchlimm
Pinterest: www.Pinterest.com/JohnSchlimm
Instagram: www.Instagram.com/JohnSchlimm
YouTube: www.YouTube.com/JohnSchlimm
More information: www.JohnSchlimm.com

Story Permissions

The Unity Mural © 2012 Nada Abdallah
Jumping Over Obstacles © 2012 Natasha Abdin
One Thing Leads to Another © 2012 Cortez Alexander
When is Power Most Powerful? © 2012 Maher Alhaj
Kilimanjaro for a Cause! © 2012 Tyler Armstrong
Birke on the Farm © 2012 Donald Birke Baehr
Blossom Power! © 2012 Aspen Bellefeuille
Mission: Help Our Troops Call Home © 2012 Brittany Anna Bergquist
Start Early and Learn for a Lifetime © 2012 Karen Carajalino
Start Early and Learn for a Lifetime © 2012 Daniela Carvajalino
Start Early and Learn for a Lifetime © 2012 Stephanie Carvajalino
From Counted Out to Counted On © 2012 Hiawatha Peter Clemons III
One Word at a Time © 2012 Kasey Dallman
I Challenge You © 2012 Katherine Claire Dildy
Changing the World, Heart to Heart © 2012 Ana Dodson
How I Found My Voice © 2012 Susan Elizabeth Doyens
The Gift of a True Friend © 2012 Lindsey Carol Eaton
Blossom Power! © 2012 Joan Elizabeth Ellis
A Better World by the Bagful © 2012 Anne Cathleen Foskett
My SWT Life © 2012 Syreeta Gates
The Luck of the Draw © 2012 Isabella Gelfand
The Rainbow Salad © 2012 Kirsten Deborah Gerbatsch
Braille the Universe! © 2012 Joshua Goldenberg
The Journey to Equality © 2012 Giovanna Guarnieri
Empower Orphans © 2012 Neha Gupta
Speak Up and Step Out! © 2012 Delaitre Jordan Hollinger
Ryan's Well © 2012 Ryan Hreljac
Social Justice for All! © 2012 Samantha Huffman
The Million Girl Revolution © 2013 Dallas Jessup
Alive and Kicking © 2012 David M. Kapata
When Strangers Become Family © 2012 Hannah Katz
Shifting the World, Little by Little © 2012 Lexi Kelley
We are Today's Leaders © 2012 Daniel Kent
YOU Can Make a Difference © 2011 Ashlee Dorisa Kephart
Be a Boss—For Real! © 2012 Seong Wook Kim
The Scholar © 2012 Chelsea Kirk
Fixing Broken Hearts © 2012 Sarah Kladar
The Big Sleep Out © 2012 Peter Larson
You Can Be Greater than You Know How to Be © 2012 Talia Yael Leman
Living on the Wild Side © 2012 Janine Licare
Advocating through Friendship © 2012 Danielle Marie Liebl
Making Spirits Bright © 2012 Raymond M. Mohler
Because She is a Girl © 2012 Sarah Musa
Blossom Power! © 2012 Roweena Naidoo
The Sea Olympics © 2012 Nathan Neff
Blossom Power! © 2012 Aleksandrina Nikifarava

Destiny's Peanuts © 2012 Abigail Parry Phillips
Blossom Power! © 2012 Jordan Elizabeth Pittman
OMG! © 2013 Carter Ries
OMG! © 2013 Olivia Ries
Stopping Hate in Its Tracks © 2011 Emily-Anne Rigal
Legislating Change © 2012 Carrie Sandstrom
Being Cool is Overrated © 2012 Arielle Schacter
What's in Your Water? © 2012 Jordyn Schara
My Sister Alex and Her Lemonade Stand © 2011 Patrick Scott
Standing Up for Animals © 2012 Paul Shapiro
Blossom Power! © 2012 Marissa Shevins
My Friend Mischa © 2012 Jeffrey Shrensel
Together We are Stronger © 2012 Ashley Shuyler
The Power of "We" © 2012 Mariah Smiley
Advocating through Friendship © 2012 Kaitlyn Smith
Toys to the Rescue! © 2012 Ashlee Kristine Smith
There is a Plan for Each of Us © 2012 Tanner James Smith
A Life Worth Living © 2012 John Franklin Stephens
Where Does Meat Come From? © 2012 Mariama Taifu-Seitu
The World Lies in the Hands of a Girl © 2012 Sophia Tareen
The World Lies in the Hands of a Girl © 2012 Nadia Tareen
Turning Green © 2012 Sabine Teyssier
Another World is Possible © 2012 Joseph Jonah Terrien
FO(u)R Fragile Hearts © 2012 Charles Maceo Thornhill
Soldier On! © 2012 Kameron Tyson
How Soccer Will Save the World © 2012 Kyle Weiss
Blossom Power! © 2012 Abigail Whitmore
Adversity = Opportunity © 2012 Claire Wineland
From Our Field to Yours © 2011 Olivia Wong

Photo Permissions

Except as indicated below, the photos in this book were provided by the story contributors and used with their permission.

Page 12 provided by Carly Hirschberg
Page 38 provided by Richard Spivey, Jr.
Page 92 provided by Blaser Photography
Page 123 provided by Jack Mazurek
Page 167 provided by The Humane Society of the United States
Page 174 provided by Denise Lett
Page 177 provided by Kim Klein
Page 184 provided by Russell Frederick
Page 201 provided by Michael P. Schultz
Page 204 provided by Angus Kennedy
Page 207 provided by Barbara Meuller
Page 239 provided by Leon County Board of Commissioners

STAND UP, AGAIN!

Publishing Syndicate and John Schlimm are now accepting stories by young activists, age 25 and under, for the sequel to *Stand Up!*—***Stand Up, Again!***

As you've seen on these pages, young people, including YOU, have the unique power to change the world like no one else.

Stand Up, Again! will continue to celebrate young people as activists and advocates who have let their voices and actions ROCK the causes and issues most important to them in their schools, their communities and around the world.

Chapters will include
topics and issues such as:

- The environment
- Human rights
- Animals
- Education
- LGBTQ
- Homelessnes
- Fitness/healthy lifestyles
- Diseases and other health issues
- Disabilities

- The military
- The arts (dancing, act-ing, writing, visual arts)
- Gun rights/control
- Bullying
- Politics
- Freedom of speech
- International issues
- And more!

Royalties will be paid to those whose stories are selected for publication. Stories should be 500–1,000 words long. For more information and to read the submission guidelines, please visit the website below.

And tell your friends, too!

www.PublishingSyndicate.com

Do you have a great teen story to share?

OMG! My Reality! For Teens

Publishing Syndicate is accepting stories for its newest teen book: *OMG! My Reality! For Teens!*

This new book will feature funny, inspiring and thoughtful real-life stories written by individuals 25 years old and younger about all aspects of teen life.

If you have a story to share, please submit it. Those whose stories are published will receive a complimentary book, T-shirt and royalties. And having a story published in a book is great for job resumes and college applications!

For guidelines, visit our website!

www.PublishingSyndicate.com

Notes

Notes

Notes

Notes

Notes

Do you have a great teen story to share?

OMG! My Reality! For Teens

Publishing Syndicate is accepting stories for its newest teen book: *OMG! My Reality! For Teens*!

This new book will feature funny, inspiring and thoughtful real-life stories written by individuals 25 years old and younger about all aspects of teen life.

If you have a story to share, please submit it. Those whose stories are published will receive a complimentary book, T-shirt and royalties. And having a story published in a book is great for job resumes and college applications!

For guidelines, visit our website!

www.PublishingSyndicate.com